BUMPY ROAD

CHALLENGES OF CIVIL WARS OF SUDAN AND SOUTH SUDAN

MARTINO KUNJOK ATEM

authorHOUSE®

AuthorHouse™
1663 Liberty Drive
Bloomington, IN 47403
www.authorhouse.com
Phone: 1 (800) 839-8640

Published by AuthorHouse 01/16/2018

ISBN: 978-1-5246-9049-6 (sc)
ISBN: 978-1-5246-9048-9 (e)

Library of Congress Control Number: 2017906774

Print information available on the last page.

This book is printed on acid-free paper.

Contents

Acknowledgements

I thank my father for teaching me to never give up hope, even in the darkest and most desperate moments of life. My appreciation goes to my mother, who single-handedly carried the load for our family after my father's premature death. To my wife Aluel Kondok and our children, thank you for letting me use your time to write this book. I also thank Abraham Atem Aguer for his constant encouragement and unwavering support, without which I would not be where I am today. Thanks to Dr. Ring De Ciman, for editing the final manuscript.

I thank the Roman Catholic Diocese of Khartoum, Sudan for giving me the education that I would not have had otherwise, in particular His Eminence Cardinal Gabriel Zubeir Wako, who encouraged me to continue my studies after deciding not to enter the priesthood. I am grateful to Sister Lina for her encouragement and support when I was in seminary.

I am indebted to Canada and to the people of Saskatchewan, "Rider Nation," for the assistance I have received since I arrived in Regina, which is on Treaty Four Territory. I appreciate the University of Regina for offering me a scholarship through the World University Service of Canada. World University Service of Canada allowed me to attend post-secondary education after the civil war in Sudan robbed me of the opportunity.

It would be impossible to thank all of the people who have helped me, directly or indirectly, along the way, so my payback to you is to help others who are less fortunate whenever I can.

In one of his speeches, former President of the United States of America Barack Obama reminds us that we are responsible for our own destiny. I would add, however, that we cannot write our destinies without the support of others. I have written and continue to write my destiny with the assistance I receive from my family members, relatives, friends, and people of good will. Thanks to all.

DEDICATION

I dedicate this book to my father. I also dedicate it to my two sisters, Nyanwai and Nyariak, who passed on in Abyei in 1988 due to a cholera outbreak that killed tens of thousands of people. This outbreak was totally preventable had the Sudanese government of the day been interested in helping the southern Sudanese people.

Last but not least, I dedicate this book to my cousin, Manut Akok Athuai, who was killed on September 1, 2016, in an avoidable civil war in the Republic of South Sudan. Like thousands of other deaths, Manut's death cannot be justified. There was no reason for a civil war after South Sudan achieved independence. It is unfortunate that the current civil war in South Sudan is mainly power struggle within the SPLM, the ruling party. Some SPLM politicians suffer from "Entitlement Syndrome". These politicians believe that they own South Sudan, and so they are using their tribal bases to either stay in power or to get into power. Regrettably, the hopes and dreams of South Sudanese had when they got their independence are turned into nightmares by these politicians.

Manut Akok Athuai

Acronyms and Terms

AAA: Addis Ababa Agreement that ended Sudan first civil war in February 1972

Allah: Arabic word for God.

AnyNya 1: First South Sudan Movement/Army that waged war between 1955- 1972.

Baggara: Arab tribe that shares borders with South Sudan, Dinka Nyok, and Malual.

Bride wealth: marriage payment made by a groom and his families and relatives to the families and relatives of the bride to legalize a marriage.

Comoboni: name given to schools run by churches in the Sudan.

IDPs: Internal Displaced Persons.

Infidel: Non-believer/non-Muslim

Halal: an Islamic religious word that means permitted by Allah.

Jihad: the government of Sudan used it exclusively to mean "A holy war against infidels in defense of Islam." The alternate meaning of "A personal struggle in devotion to

Islam. The alternate meaning of Jihad is personal struggle in devotion to Islam.

Luak: thatched mud building bigger than a hut and usually used for keeping cattle in at night.

LWF: Lutheran World Federation.

Moon: Dinka word referring to bulls, oxen, and people that were paid to the SPLM/A as taxes in Sudan's civil wars.

Mujihadeen: militias recruited and supported by the Sudan government to fight Jihad in South Sudan.

Murrahaleen: tribal armed Arab militias that raided villages, killed people, looted cattle, and took children and women into slavery.

NCP: Sudan National Congress Party.

Nhialic Wa: Dinka word for God of my father.

Polygamy: a practice or custom in which a man has more than one wife at the same time.

Razayqat: an Arab tribe that shares border with Dinka Ngok and Malual Dinka.

Shahadah: Means "the testimony" and is an Islamic creed declaring belief in the oneness of God and the acceptance of Muhammad as God's prophet.

SPLM: Sudan People's Liberation Movement (the political wing of the SPLA)

SPLA: Sudan People's Liberation Army (the military wing of the SPLM)

Thoi: Fishing bucket made of sticks.

UNHCR: United Nations High Commission for Refugees.

WFP: World Food Program.

World Vision: a non-profit organization (Non-governmental).

WUSC: World University Service of Canada

Introduction

No one can give an accurate count of those
who have died from bullets, malnutrition,
or neglect on the part of the government of
the Sudan, many of those leaders have been
pleased to see the demise of their Sudanese
African brothers. [1]

Sudan's civil wars profoundly changed my life.
Although the main reason for this book is to tell my life's
story, it is not possible to do so without also discussing
Sudan's politics and the conflict that made my life what it
has been. Both of Sudan's civil wars, which took place from
1955—1972 and 1983—2005, shattered my family's lives.
The social, economic, religious, and political turmoil in the
Sudan shaped my life to be what it is today. The stories told
here are mine, unless indicated otherwise. I tell them as I
recall them. Some of these events occurred over thirty years
ago when I was very young and illiterate. Other aspects of
this story are ongoing, such as the implications of my status
as a citizen of both South Sudan and Canada.

Southern Sudanese and Northern Sudanese had little
in common. It was a mistake of the British colonizers to

---

[1] J. Millard Burr and Robert O. Collins. Requiem for the Sudan:
War, Drought, and Disaster Relief on the Nile, 1995, p. 1

hand power over both jurisdictions to Northerners under a united Sudan on January 1st, 1956. Prior to colonization and after, the northern leaders wanted every Sudanese person to embrace political Islam and Arabic culture, with the reality of multi-ethnic, multi-cultural and multi-religious Sudan. Political Islam was a tool used by northern elites to undermine diversity and Islamize the whole of Sudan. As a southern Sudanese politician explained, "The idea of secular power cannot find entry into the heads of such leaders [the northern Sudan governing elite], because secularism, to them, means willfully allowing society into committing acts of immorality."[2] This political Islam was tyrannical, misrepresenting true Islam and its teachings.

Non-Muslims in Sudan rejected Arab culture and repressive political Islam. For five decades, oppressive regimes in Khartoum tried to crush all resistance. This created an environment of mistrust, exploitation, slavery, and the destruction of properties and lives. Sudan was engulfed in two brutal civil wars that lasted over three decades because of these beliefs. As a result, more than three million Sudanese people died and roughly three million more were internally or externally displaced.

The rebellion my father participated in would be remembered as Anynya 1. It would be followed by Anynya 2, which morphed into the Sudan People's Liberation Movement/Army. My father actively participated in the Sudan's first civil war waged by AnyNya movement. That

---

[2] Albino, Oliver B. Power and Democracy in the Sudan How Decentralization Hurts, 2006, p. 82.

war lasted for about seventeen years, and it was concluded by an agreement signed in Addis Ababa between the Sudan government and the AnyNya movement. However, my father and some southern rebels rejected the agreement. As a result, the government of the Sudan took all the cattle from my grandfather, Atem Majok. My father refusal to accept the agreement what resulted taking of his father cattle permanently damaged the relationship between my grandfather and father, a relationship that was still unhealed when my grandfather died. On his deathbed, my grandfather handed over a blessing spear to my mother. The spear was to be given to me when I grew up. The blessed spear was to be my protector.

I vividly remember when I asked my father about the spear my mother told me that my grandfather left for me. My father response was that the spear was a symbol of your grandfather's spirit hovering over us. He said, "My father was very upset with me because I did not surrender to the government. However, he was pleased that his name and linage will continue through you". My father kept quiet for a while before he utter any word, then he said, "My son, I wish I had accepted my father's advice and gave in. Look, I eventually accepted the defeat of the Arabs and I surrendered after my father's death. I am glad your mother was presence when my father joined our ancestors. I know I will not live long given the way my war injuries are deteriorating."

My father himself died shortly after the second civil war began. When he was near death, he poured cow's milk on my palm. This signified that I was taking over family's responsibilities as he was joining our ancestors.

Southern Sudanese and some other marginalized Sudanese took up arms against the Sudanese government in 1983. This same civil war is internationally reported to have left two and a half million dead and over four million homeless. I believe the real numbers are higher. Like many Southern Sudanese, I was internally displaced before I became a refugee searching for safety and opportunities.

During Sudan's second civil war, Arab tribal militias captured many young South Sudanese and sold them into slavery. Other youth went to neighboring countries to join the movement. Some were conscripted into the Sudan People's Liberation Movement/Army (SPLM/A) against their will. These boys were known as the "Red Army." They trained in Ethiopia because Ethiopian Prime Minister, Mengistu Haile Mariam, was one of a few leaders who supported the SPLM/A from its inception. As they were on their way to Ethiopia, the Sudanese government relentlessly bombed these youth as they tiptoed among landmines and wild animals. This act left permanent physical and emotional scars for all who experienced it.

Like the remaining Southerners who did not leave for other countries, I was forced to go to Northern Sudan. There, we were treated like foreigners in our own country. We were put into camps with meagre food, stagnant water, and hardly any shelter. Searching for safety and a better life, thousands of Southern Sudanese became cheap laborers and house servants for the northerners. I, too, became a domestic worker for over four years. I acted on my father's advice not to give up any hope even in darkest moments and so I began to attend evening school.

Bumpy Road is a book about the effects of Sudan's civil wars on my family, my spiritual journey from Atemyath to Christianity, and from being South Sudanese to being Canadian. The book talks about the paradox of embracing Dinka beliefs and Christian beliefs as well. In an attempt to reconcile these dichotomies, I describe myself as "a self-appointed ambassador" who equally defends the Dinka religion and Christianity, Dinka values and Canadian values. My response to the tragic attack on Wau town on January 29th, 1998, demonstrated my belief in both Christianity and my Dinka religion. As I ran for dear life, I called upon both Atamyath and Jesus Christ. I do not know who answered my prayers, but one thing I know for sure, is that I am alive and well today, whereas many people did not make it through that fatal day.

The challenges I encountered along the way on my life journey have become sources of my strength, audacity, and willpower for optimism. The first Sudan's civil war destroyed relationships between my father and his father, whereas the second civil war internally displaced me and made me a refugee. Out of all these calamities, I was able to go to school and also acquire Canadian citizenship, which both are blessings and challenges. It is a blessing to raise my children in a peaceful developed nation. It is a challenge to reconcile culture of my adopted country, Canada, with the culture of Dinka, as well as harmonizing my ancestors' religion with Christianity.

However, these challenges of reconciling Dinka's culture with Western culture and harmonizing Dinka's Traditional Religion with Christianity are nothing compare with the pain I feel about my country of origin, Republic of South Sudan that SPLM party politicians have turned into a killing field. South Sudanese tolerated corruption, nepotism, as well as lack of services delivery, but tribal and regional enmities resulting from South Sudan's civil war became unbearable. Neither Dinka, Nuer, nor Equatorians are the problem in South Sudan, but the failed policies of the ruling SPLM party and their broke way former SPLM who still called themselves SPLM in Opposition are the problem. SPLM in South Sudan is like Political Islam and Arabism in the Sudan.

CHAPTER 1

THE BRUTAL DIVORCE OF SOUTH SUDAN AND THE SUDAN

> The dream of a united Sudan, adverse nation linking the Arab World to Sub-Saharan Africa, had evaporated like a slick of water under Sudanese Sun. [3]

Religious discord and political marginalization were among the reasons for South Sudan and the Sudan's incomplete divorce. The separation is incomplete because there are a few disputed areas that belong neither to South Sudan nor to the Sudan according to current maps of the two countries. From time immemorial, Northern Sudan was different from Southern Sudan in many respects, including religion, lineage, and geographical characteristics. Despite these differences, the Northern Sudanese political elite attempted to force the Southern Sudanese to embrace political Islam and Arabic culture. This manifestation of political Islam had no room for separation between religion and state. This state of affairs created a lack of social cohesion, tolerance, and peaceful con-existence between

---

[3] Copnall, James. A Poisonous Thorn in Our Hearts: Sudan and South Sudan's Bitter and Incomplete Divorce. P. 1

non-Muslims and political Muslims in the Sudan. The southern Sudanese resistance against this enforced new order and the consequent economic and political marginalization resulted in Sudan's civil wars.

Even before Sudan gained independence from Britain, Southern Sudan and Northern Sudan had different cultures and religions. The Northern Sudanese were predominately Muslims, while the Southern Sudanese were either Christians or animists. The majority of southern Sudanese who were less educated believed in the African traditional religions of their ancestors. The educated and the elite southern Sudanese were Christians. Southern Sudanese who refused to embrace Islam but continued to practice their African culture and religion, or who embraced Christianity, were labeled infidels and inferior to the Northern Sudanese Muslims who now held power.

Prior to the independence of the Sudan, Northern Sudanese were more educated than Southern Sudanese. This was a primary reason they were granted power from Great Britain after independence was granted on January 1, 1956. Unfortunately, the elite of Northern Sudan who dominated professional and political life had no tolerance for the non-Muslims and non-Arabs in the Sudan.

Whether Christian or African religions believers, Southern Sudanese totally opposed this imposed ideology in its totality and fought in both civil wars for self-rule. The leadership of the Sudan People's Liberation Movement/ Army wanted a "New Sudan" that would accommodate Sudan's diversity within a framework of equality, without discrimination on the basis of race, ethnicity, religion, culture, or gender. This New Sudan ideology could not prevail in the North, so Southern Sudan chose independence over a unity based on political Islam.

The Northern ruling elite who assumed power after Britain left tried to impose political Islam and Arabic culture on non-Arabs and non-Muslims in the South. The Arabic language was made a national and official language, and Islam was also made the national religion. This policy denied the language and religion rights of non-Arabs and non-Muslims, which led to a determined resistance in the South. There was no compromise, and as a result, these incompatibilities triggered two devastating civil wars.

The Northern Sudanese elites had an unfounded and unsubstantiated belief in the superiority of their own beliefs. To them, the only way to bring the Southern Sudanese to equal status with the Northern Sudanese was through Political Islam and Arabic culture. If the South Sudanese embraced Islam and Arabic culture, the Northern elites believed, then and only then would they be equal. Islam and Arabic culture were deemed superior to African traditional religions, African culture, and Christianity. Christianity in the South had replaced African animism but neither were acceptable to Islamists. Civil war was the predictable result of this incompatible marriage between an Islamic North and a non-Islamic South.

The strategies of the governing elite made Islam, as well as Arabic culture and traditions, synonymous with the name "Sudan." There was no separation between religion and state, which led to a misrepresentation of the Islam found in the Holy Qur'an. Not only was Islam made a national religion despite the diversity of the Sudanese people, Islam was also implicitly used as a way for opportunistic people to attain job opportunities. Some Southern Sudanese who embraced Islam did not convert to the actual teaching of Islam. Instead, they would work in mosques, but meanwhile say in secret that they are not really Muslims — something very insulting to Islamic belief.

One of the well-known stories of "conversion" for convenience belongs to Deng. He is a Dinka man who changed his name to Mohammed when he converted into Islam in the 1990s. At the beginning of his journey to Islam, Deng attended Mosque on Fridays. After a few months as a Muslim, Deng privately told some of his close friends and family members that he was not a true Muslim in the real sense. Some of his Muslim friends became suspicious when he also began attend St. Matthew's Cathedral Roman Catholic Church in Khartoum every Sunday.

As time went on, Deng became a regular churchgoer. His Dinka friend, Chol, was worried about his friend's state of mind. One Sunday, Chol saw Deng in the church and so he approached him and asked what he was doing in the church. Deng responded that he went to Mosque on Fridays because he got paid. He told Chol that he works in the mosque.

Chol was confused and did not understand what his friend meant. Chol asked Deng to explain what he meant. Deng said, "Come on, Chol, do not be ridiculous. I have a family to feed and no job. I have four wives and sixteen children, to be exact. No manna from heaven anymore. I get paid when I go to the mosque by my Muslim friends, and I have a good job as a result of my new faith." Deng continued, saying, "On Sundays, I go to church to pray." His friend was left speechless, yet he understood the situation. At the time, life was very hard for Southerners who had moved to Khartoum.

As Deng's good friend, Chol invited Deng (Mohammed) and few of their friends for dinner at his house. As a custom, Dinka people share even the little things they have. Even though Chol had no job, he instructed one of his wives to prepare a meal for his friends because they had a very important issue to discuss. Chol and his family were living in unfinished apartments. Most Dinka people who could not afford to rent houses or apartments to live in used unfinished apartments for free because, the men were considered watchmen for those apartments and houses.

Chol's wife agreed and cooked a nice meal with the money she made from brewing and selling local wine. Chol announced the purpose of the invitation, something already known by close friends Lual and Majak — friends who, together with Chol, urged Deng to abandon Islam. Deng heard them out, cleared his voice, and took his turn.

When Deng spoke, he always spoke with passion, very loudly and intimidatingly. Deng thanked his friend Chol for the meal, which was not normal for Dinka culture except under Arabic or western influences. In Dinka, food is considered to be a dead thing, so when one has it, one

5

shares it with others. Deng began, "Let me be clear to all of you fools." He did not call them fools to put them down but because they were close friends who joked a lot. Deng continued, "Your families are depending on little incomes from your wives brewing local beer, which sometimes puts your wives at risk from the police because alcohol is illegal in this country. Even Allah will never punish me. What I get from my Muslim friends is Halal, legal according to Islam. If there is a heaven, I have more chances to go to heaven than the three of you here."

"Allah will forgive my sins," Deng carried on, "because I pray five times a day and I go to Mosque on Fridays. Prophet Muhammad, peace be upon him, will be my witness on this. Islam and Christianity both teach us to take care of our families. I am doing my duties as head of my family." Lual laughed, but he was rebuked by Majak, who said, "This is not a laughing matter."

Deng smiled and asserted, "If I appear before Jesus when I die, Jesus will also defend me because I attend church and pray every Sunday." Deng declared, "Let me be pragmatic: I am doing this to avoid mistreatments of my wives by the city police. We all know that our women are humiliated whenever they brew local beer just to feed their families. Chol, I get your concern, my friend, but I have few options in this country. I have to pay for my children's school fees. You should know that, because of what we are talking about here, my children are going to good schools, while many Southern Sudanese children do child labor. This is all about survival, my friends." Deng grinned, stating, "I rest my case".

Majak, the last friend to speak, said, "This is a result of the war waged by the governing Northern elite urging Northern Muslims to fight us, the so-called infidels. We are all aware that the Sudanese government is favoring Muslim Sudanese over non-Muslims".

Majak concluded, "I think Deng is making sense. Who are we to judge? Both religions are foreign to us. Neither Christianity nor Islam is a Dinka religion. We have abandoned our "gods" and embraced these "foreign gods" and now we are trying to discourage someone smart enough to feed his children." He turned to Deng and said, "Please give us some money for transport. I will think about joining you, brother Deng, and if Atemwa gets angry with me, I will tell him that you said, *'Atem aya mat ke rok,'* which translates *you cannot leave your luak open and say Atemwa will protect my cattle from hyena.* It is the flip side of the English adage, 'God helps those who help themselves,' and says you can't expect God to help those who refuse."

Deng jumped in and said, "Remember the story, guys?"

Majak asked, "What story?"

Deng reminded them of the story that when *Aciek*, the Creator, created the world, a white man, an Arab man, and a black man went to see the Creator. The Creator asked them what they wanted before they left the Garden of Eden. The white man said, "I want a spirit of innovation and creativity to invent things". The Creator said, "It will be done as you wish." The Creator asked the Arab man what he wanted. The Arab man replied, "I want wealth." The Creator said, "Your wish is done, and your land will be filled with oil." Then the Creator turned to the black man and asked what he wanted. The black man said, "Oh, I'm just here with my bros." When Deng reached the punchline, everyone burst into laughter because they all heard this joke before.

Deng asked them why the black man didn't want anything. No answer. Deng added some details not in the myth explaining why black people are poor. He said, "When the Creator smiled at the black man's response that he was just there with his brothers, the black man declared, 'I want to witness their choices and become their judge when they begin to fight. The inventor may want to invent strong weapons to take the wealth of the Arab man. I will remind the white man what you, the Creator gave him. Also, if the Arab man were to use his wealth to invent weapons competitions, I will be your witness and will remind him of his choice.'" Deng said, "You see, brothers, we are peace-makers and we should be so."

Lual interrupted and said, "I think these Arab elites and some western religions are stronger than our forefathers' religions. We are content with whatever we have." The three friends dismissed the joke, changed the subject, and kept talking until late, when Deng, Lual, and Majak had to leave to catch the transport. Lual was going to Jaborana, Deng was going to Khartoum-North, and Majak had to go to Jebel Aulia. All these places were internally displaced persons' camps, where they lived.

Before they leave, Chol took a turn and said, "That is why our Nhialic neither require us to convert others to our religion nor does he require us to defend him. We care for one another. We are our brothers' and sisters' keepers." He continued, saying, "You see some white people are individualistic and Arab elites will do anything to acquire wealth." Chol added, "Christianity preaches about a person going to heaven or hell, and Islam preaches the same. He asserted, "Most of Sudanese elites' social status are based on how much wealth they have while some people in the West measure their successes by their inventions." He said, "For us black people, we either go to heaven together with our family members or we go to hell together." Chol finished his statement, saying, "Our Nhialic does not require our protection." Of course, Chol had never visited another country and generalizations are normal to make.

Chol's statement about protecting Nhialic refers to the notion of fighting infidels, that is, non-Muslims. The Sudanese government compelled young men to join jihad when it could not defeat the SPLM/A. The acts of the government did not match with the true faith of Islam and the teaching of the Holy Qur'ran.

For instance, at the beginning of the 1990s, Dr. Hassan al Turabi, a world-renowned Islamic scholar who brought Omar Hassan al Beshir to power in 1989, issued keys to new Mujahidin graduates. These young men were promised Paradise if they killed the infidel SPLA soldiers. A few times,

SPLA soldiers captured Sudanese soldiers, amputated their limbs, and sent them back to Khartoum to tell Beshir and Turabi that the SPLM/A was implementing Islamic Sharia law in the war-zones. Of course, amputation was the penalty for theft under Sharia law, and this was just what the SPLM/A thought of government forces stealing land that did not belong to them. The rulers were not occupying empty territory, but people's properties.

Sudan's first civil war officially began on August 18, 1955, and ended February 27, 1972. This war cost many lives and properties, especially in the south. The second civil war formally began on May 16, 1983, and ended on January 9, 2005. After two decades of fighting, the SPLM/A and the ruling Sudan National Congress Party (NCP) realized that the war was unwinnable, so they sought a political settlement. With support from international bodies, both parties signed a Comprehensive Peace Agreement (CPA). As part of this agreement, the southern Sudanese were given a choice between unity and separation after six years. When that time passed, the Southern Sudanese made an overwhelming choice to secede.

In fact, according to (source), "Both the AAA and the CPA attempted to accommodate the evolving conception of Northern and Southern Sudanese national identity. The agreements are testimonies to Sudan's difficulty transcending its regional identities".[4] The failure of the Northern Sudanese elites to make unity attractive moved over ninety eight

---

[4] Leach, p. 36

per cent of the Southern Sudanese population to vote for secession on January 9, 2011.

Republic of South Sudan shares borders with six African countries, which are: Central Republic of Africa, Democratic Republic of Congo, Republic of Ethiop, Kenya, Uganda and the Republic of Sudan. The borders between the Republic of the Sudan and Republic of South Sudan have some unresolved issues like Abyei, and Panthou among others.

Although the vote to secede was honored with independence, the resolution was not yet complete. The civil wars ended in a brutal, incomplete divorce, as illustrated by James Copnall's book, *A Poisonous Thorn in Our Hearts: Sudan and South Sudan's Bitter and Incomplete Divorce*, leaving the Republic of South Sudan and the Sudan as countries with four major disputed areas.

CHAPTER 2

MY FATHER IN THE SUDAN'S CIVIL WAR

Give this spear to Atem when he is old enough. This is my blessing. He will carry on my name.

My father took up arms and fought against Arab's discrimination and marginalization of non-Muslims and non-Arab Sudanese in the first Sudanese civil war, known as Anynya 1. When the Addis Abba Agreement was signed between the Anynya 1 movement and the Sudanese government, my father did not honor the agreement. Consequently, the government of Sudan took his father's cattle, my grandfather's, to force my father to surrender. My father still refused, which led to unhealthy relations between him and his father, Atem Majok as well as father's difficulty to pay the bride wealth for my mother. I grew up in a village where every adult was a guardian of the community. I was very young when my loving father passed on. It was not only a social and cultural obligation, but also a moral obligation for me to break the ground for the burial. Also, I was socially, culturally, and morally obliged to put the first dirt into the grave of my father to seal the border between his earthly life and our ancestors' world that he joined.

My mother is from Paguor, a clan whose totem is a lion and pumpkin. I think that the Western Halloween Feast and my mother's clan respect to lion may have something in common. My maternal relatives, my mother, my sisters and I do not eat pumpkins because they represent the lion. Pumpkins are considered sacred.

I never saw or knew of anyone who killed a lion with their bare hands as some of my colleagues and friends from Canada often ask. I did, however, see people killing lions using spears. I remember well when hunters came to our house in pursuit of a wounded lion. My father gave them the wrong direction. Our neighbor, Uncle Atem Maktung, later told the hunters that the lion was sacred for my mother's clan. Uncle Atem Maktung directed hunters to direction of the lion's direction, which made my father very upset. Unfortunately, the hunters followed Atem Maktung's advice and when they came face to face with the speared lion, they threw more spears at the hurt animal.

Unfortunately, the wounded lion killed one hunter and injured four. The killed hunter was a friend to my uncle Mabong. I had lot of nightmares about the incident because I saw the dead man full of blood with some body parts missing or unrecognizable.

Few days later, I asked my dad why he wanted to mislead the hunters. My father told me that he did not want anyone to be killed or maimed by the wounded lion. He explained, "The animal was badly wounded and should be left to die alone." These were some of the lessons I learned from my father before the result of the wars took its toll on the family.

Despite negative effects of the war on my family, especially on relations between my father and grandfather, I was deeply loved by both my father and grandfather as well as by the whole family. In this unconditional love, I found acceptance, approval, praise, and security. My loving grandparents and parents were more than a blessing to me: they were a phenomenal inspiration.

Children like me, who were born in remote areas of southern Sudan without schools, never celebrate birthdays. We remember and cherish good events and avoid remembering bad ones. My native language, Dinka, does not have a phrase or a word for "happy birthday." I do not celebrate my birthday, because I do not know my date of birth, nor do many people of my generation from my village.

Most South Sudanese who migrate to the Western World are forced by their new adopted country to come up with a date of birth, which in most cases turns out to be January 1st. That is why in the United States of America, the Lost Boys and Lost Girls from the Sudan celebrate a joint birthday on January 1st every year. What a brilliant idea! The western system forces us to make up a date of birth for documents, which has consequences, such as when to retire. Those of us from Southern Sudan who reduced our ages significantly for resettlement purposes will have to work over the retirement age.

I was born and raised in a thatch-roofed hut. Even now, people still live in thatch-roofed huts, even though some villagers now have cell phones. My parents did their best to raise us. We never lacked anything that any child in our village had. Our family's business, combined with a little farming, were the main source of our income and livelihood.

Neither birth certificates nor death certificates existed when I was born. Therefore, I do not know the dates for my father's birth nor for his death. After I went to school, I began to date my father's death to 1984, but I still can't guess which month. One of the regrettable things about my father's death is that I do not have any pictures of him. I can only hope that he had a picture taken while in the Congo that I could one day see. When my children ask to see my father's picture, I cannot well explain to them why he did not have a picture.

My father was a soldier who never trusted the Arab leaders of the Sudan and badly wanted independence for the South. My father did not know his age when he entered the movement, only that he was a young man like most of his colleagues. My father fought for the freedom of his countrymen and countrywomen. The war was the first attempt by South Sudanese to separate from North Sudan. He did not like the peace accord which ended the war, known to the Sudanese as the Addis Ababa Agreement (AAA). My father used to talk to me about the war, calling the agreement "cowardice surrender" when I was about eight or nine years old. The leaders of the movement signed an agreement that was never honored.

My father, like some South Sudanese, did not believe in the Addis Ababa peace accord of 1972, but they had no power to collectively violate it. The failed agreement proved my father right when he felt betrayed by his own leaders, who signed a peace deal that did not last, nor did it solve any of their problems. Those who refused to return to Sudan after the signing of the agreement were hunted down by the government, including their former comrades in arms who later became government officials.

One day, a South Sudanese man came to my grandfather in his cattle camp and asked him to send for my father to have him surrender. My grandfather was threatened to surrender his son, or else his cattle would be taken away from him forever. My grandfather did as demanded by the Sudan government soldiers, but my father refused to surrender himself. The army, led by the South Sudanese man, decided to take my grandfather's cattle. My grandfather was given three days to turn in his son, my father, or he would not get his cattle back.

My father rejected his father's call to surrender to the government soldiers, but instead went and sought after the man who took his father's cattle. My dad ordered for the arrest of the man who had taken his father's cattle, and the man was executed. There was no judge, yet the order was carried out. My grandfather's cattle were never returned. Losing his father's cattle made my father a poor man, as every man's wealth is measured in the number of cattle he owns. Therefore, my father could not afford to pay the number of the cattle required to marry when the time came for him to take a wife.

When my father fell in love with my mother and wanted to marry her, my wealthy maternal family wanted a high price for their daughter, but since my grandfather's cattle were never returned, they did not want my father. With the few cattle that my father gathered and support from his relatives and friends, he paid the bride-price. Despite the resistance from his future in-laws, my father overcame my maternal family's unreasonable bride-price demanded, and managed to marry my mother by obligation in the end.

My father wanted me to get an education, but he did not put me in school because there was no school in Agok Adiang, Twic County. There was a missionary school run by the Roman Catholic Church in Mayen Abun, but it was far away from our home. However, my father taught me that you do not have to be wealthy to create your own life.

Like thousands of his fellow southern Sudanese, my father joined the movement called Anynya 1. The word "Anynya" originated from one of the local languages in Equatoria, and it loosely means "snake poison." The name was meant to show that despite their inferior arms against the well-armed forces of government of Sudan, the Anynya would bite and win. The Anynya movement resisted for about seventeen years until the Khartoum regime signed the peace agreement with the Anynya.

My father told me that in most cases during the war, a single rifle was supported by many men carrying spears fighting against the well-armed soldiers. Having heard this story many times, I conclusion that the Anynya 1 proved the saying, "Where there is a will, there is a way," beyond a doubt. The Anynya was able to negotiate a political settlement with the Sudanese government of the day at the time when some members of Anynya thought they had good chance of negotiating a better deal if the leadership was to wait for few months.

My father got sick from a bullet wound he sustained during the war. When he was finally captured by government forces, he was tortured. Fortunately, he lived beyond those sufferings. Even though I was young, I remember spending more time with my father than with other family members. Dad wanted to initiate me into family small business and to bring me up as he thought best. As his firstborn son, I would be the means by which he would live on after he died. According to the Dinka section we are from, if a man dies with a son, it is said that the man's liver is taken out. Offspring considered livers taken out of the dead person especially male offspring. The boy will continue the line and fulfill what was left unfinished.

Due to my father's lack of formal education, he did not know the year he was shot and tortured. He told me he was taken to Congo for medical treatment right after he got shot. After few months he ordered the execution of the man who betrayed his father's cattle. After my father ordered the execution of the man, he stayed in bush for few months.

I suspect he was shot in 1972 or 1973, because he managed to live in the bush for a while following the Addis Ababa Agreement. He resisted what he called Arab discrimination against non-Muslims, non-Arabs and the weakness of the Southern Sudanese leaders who accepted an outcome short of separation or independence. War wounds took my dad's life before his time. He died being bitter at the southern Sudanese politicians, whom he viewed as traitors to their people. According to my father, the Addis Ababa Agreement was a sellout, a surrender of Southerners' rights to the government of the Sudan.

The Dinka do not write wills. However, anyone who dies leaves responsibility to the first-born son in the family. The first-born son's role in Dinka society matters in all things, including inheritances, family decision-making, and even the burial of a parent.

The first-born son inherits things such as the spear of the family. If there are any sacrifices to be offered, the first-born slaughters a bull or a goat and offers the animal to the spirits. When an adult dies, it is the responsibility of the first-born son to dig the grave and then put the mud into the grave. Dinka culture has no caskets; the dead are buried in a white bed sheet. I was very young, but I'm glad that I did my duty as a first-born son, starting my father's grave and putting the first dirt inside when my father's body was properly put in the grave. This duty is an obligation of every first-born male in Dinka culture as well as some other tribes in South Sudan. The dirt that I put on my father's body in the tomb sealed the bridge between earthly life and my father's life after death. The only comfort I had after Dad's death was that he would watch over us.

I did something that my father was not able to do for his father, my grandfather. When my grandfather passed on, my father was away on a mission to Wau. After my father was captured and tortured, he was reinstated into the Sudan army. He was then sent to Wau by his commanding officer to assist with some military duty. There were no vehicles at the time, so the journey took him more than three days, and there were no phones. My grandfather had been dead for days by the time my dad arrived in Wau and my father heard the news of the death of his father few days later. My father became bitter and decided to quit the army.

I remember my mother telling me many times how upset my grandfather was when she visited him. When my mother heard that her father-in-law was about to die, she went to see him and wanted to take me there to receive blessings from him, since he is the man I am named after. However, my father's mother prevented me from going, because she was upset with her husband over his refusal to marry my father off. I wish my grandfather had lived longer so that I could have understood the conflict. When my grandfather saw my mother, he asked for me. He was furious at what my grandmother had done and offered me his blessing.

My grandfather told my mother that if she ever left the family, she should leave me behind. According to my mother, my grandfather said, "Nyadeng, do not under any circumstances take Atem with you. Atem is my name and nothing will harm him." Atem Majok, my grandfather, spat on my mother's hands and said, "These hands will never carry Atem away from this family." My grandfather then gave my mother the "Blessed Spear" for my protection. My mother promised my grandfather that no matter what, she would stay in the family and raise me. After my father's death, my mother said she would never leave Atem Majok's family because she must keep the promise she made to him.

My grandfather worried, was because there were not enough cattle to pay as bride-wealth for my mother.

My grandmother, Ajok Malith, loved me more than anything I can remember. When I was growing up in the village, spanking was the main means of discipline. If my mom or dad ever spanked me, my grandmother would protest by refusing to eat. After I grew up and remember the love from my grandmother and what my grandfather told my mother about me, I know for sure I was enclosed by love.

Life after death empowered my grandfather and my father to watch over our family members. This is a power I have no proof of, but one that I strongly believe in. The Dinka people, especially in Twic, bury their departed members in the backyard and offer them sacrifices on certain times. There is no graveyard because of the strong belief that departed loved ones watch over us after death.

After my father joined our ancestors, our moth became the sole breadwinner when my father died. Without a doubt, she filled my late father's shoes while still wearing her own shoes as a mother. Our father became our protector in the world of spirits. We believe in life after death, but in a different way from the way Islam and Christianity conceive of it. There is neither hell nor heaven. Our dead ancestors watch after their living ones.

My sisters and I could never ask for a better mother. It is because of her that I could concentrate on my education. I vividly remember people telling me how my mother fed them whenever they visited our home in the village. When

I heard those touching stories about how my mother kept the family name alive, I made it my job to become educated so that I could take proper care of her once she become old.

As a first-born son, I was socially expected to take the role that was left vacant by my father's untimely departure. Since my father did not die suddenly, every minute of his illness was a teachable moment. He taught me how to be responsible not only as a child, but especially as a man after he would be gone. When my father approached his death, he told my mother to wake me. When I came to his room, he told me today is the day. I am sure nobody including my mother understood what he meant by "Today is the day". I immediately remembered a discussion we had in Akce Nhial (Kiir River) on our way from Abyei probably summer of 1983 when the lorry that was carried our goods broken down.

My father and I ate dried fish and then two of us under a tree talked for more than two hours. My father was telling me that his health was failing him. After our discussion, he told me he was glad that he had prepared me to follow his footsteps. I had no clue what he meant, but he said, "When the day comes, I let you know". I think my father trying to hide from my mother that he was dying. I sat beside him and tears started running. My father turned to his usual way of reprimanding me, "Son of a woman." He said, "I have taught you what you need to know." He turned to my mother and asked her to give him a cup of cow milk. We had only two cows that had milk at the time. He poured milk into my palm, symbolizing the handing over of family responsibilities. Instantly, mother understood what was happening and she began wailing and our neighbors came.

In few minutes, my father joined the company of our ancestors. My father passed on, in March 1984. Months after my father's death, I began to clear a piece of land and farmed it. Sorghum cultivation in my village is done with primitive tools. I farmed that land and yielded a surplus of sorghum, which we bartered for a bull. The bull was slaughtered for my father's memorial service, which gave me pride and my mother confidence. Sacrificing that bull to my dear father was a way to pay homage to him. My father always hovers over us, his children.

Sudan second civil war intensified few months after my father joined our ancestors. The regimes that came and went during the 21 years of Sudan's civil wars consistently used hunger as a weapon against the Southern Sudanese civilians. This was one way of depriving the SPLM/A of its manpower, supports, and supplies. The SPLM/A depended largely on the food they collected from civilians. SPLM/A's soldiers neither had salaries nor did they have incentives of any sort.

The Sudan government recruited and supported Mujahedeen, Muslim militias in late 1980s. The Mujahedeen increased their raiding activities, killing innocent Southern Sudanese civilians. The government that was supposed to defend these innocent Southern Sudanese supplied the militias with weapons to indiscriminately enslave and kill them, including women and children. Dinka villages were burned to the ground, and their cattle were taken north. It is a tragedy that was neither acknowledged nor punished by the International Community.

As the civil war raged and dragged on, the famine and the brutal Mujahedeen militias assaults on Dinka people forced the Dinka to evacuate their homes and move to Northern Sudan. I am one of those Southern Sudanese who sought safety in Northern Sudan. Northern Sudanese were very kind to us Southerners, but the government was not and did not protect the civilians the South.

The majority of Twic Mayardit children who survived the brutal and barbaric war had to create their own world. Although Arab militias destroyed the Twic area, the spirit of Twic citizens became stronger than ever. Prior to Twic's annihilation, the children of Twic received the values, religion, and culture through day-to-day life. Twic County, which is now a state, will always be my home, even when I do not live there. It is where I first experienced love, care, and faith in humanity.

CHAPTER 3

TWIC COUNTY'S DESTRUCTION

The destruction of lives, properties, and culture in Twic uprooted and annihilated the basis of our spiritual, cultural, and ethnic beliefs. Our very existence as people was devastated. Our relationships with the wildlife were perpetually destroyed. Nevertheless, this destruction created unquenched determination among the Twic people to overcome these challenges. One of Twic artists, Machol Amourdit, captured it in his album, *Aci Twic Kon Gam*, a name which means, "Twic will never accept defeat and leave their home land." Twic was targeted by the government of Sudan for many reasons, the foremost being that it was the home of Kerubino, the man who triggered the Revolution on May 16th, 1983.

As this book goes to print, Twic State is comprised of six counties: Ajak of Kuac section, Akoc of Thon section, Aweng of Akuar section, Turalei of Amuol section, Pan-Nyok of Cibok section, and Wunrok of Adiang section.

Many wild animals roamed Twic County's villages. Giraffe herds were seen almost everywhere. The "king of the forest" was not only present in the stories told, but was also common in the village. I can vividly remember the beauty of Twic. Agok Adiang village in Twic was full of trees and wild animals. Gazelles, deer, rabbits, wild pigs,

25

giraffes, lions, and many other animals roamed the village. People lived simple, yet colorful lives, full of wild animals and fertile lands around them. Giraffes roamed constantly by our homes.

The Sudanese government of the day trained and armed Baggara Arab tribesmen and sent them to Twic, Northern Bahr El Ghazal, and other neighboring areas. These government militias used horses and camels to loot villages, kill strong men, and burn down anything they were not able to carry on their animals. The militias took advantage of lack of strong (SPLM-A) soldiers' presence in the area. The second civil war caused numerous and horrendous crimes against the people of Twic, like many other South Sudanese and marginalized groups in the Sudan. The civil war destroyed lives, properties and, indeed, cultures.

The catastrophe and anguish that Twic people experienced during that war have nurtured unbeatable strengths within them. Twic people have never accepted hopelessness or cynicism. Among many songs that described the effect of civil war on Twic people is artists Machol Amourdit. Referring to the destruction caused by the Murrahaleen, the song goes:

> They have burned down Ajak.
> The have burned down Aweng,
> They have burned down Turalei.
> They have burned down Mayen Abun.
> They have burned down Wunrok.
> They have burned down Pan-Nyok.
> They have burned down Akoc and

They have killed our spiritual and traditional
leader Kondokdit,
But the people of Twic will never quit their
land nor will they surrender.

Early morning November 17, 1983, Murrahaleen
attacked Twic area in all directions with their superior
modern weapons. They killed many people: children, women
and men including one of their spiritual and traditional
leaders, Kondok Makuei, known also Kondokdit. The
killing of this great Twic spiritual and traditional leader and
many people was meant to send clear message that mercy is
for the weak. The raid was also meant to destroy fabric of
Twic Mayardit, yet the outcome was opposite. Twic spirit
became strong and never allowed the land to be occupied
by others, especially the Baggara and Razaygqat tribes. This
happened about eight months after my father's death.

The Baggara raiders destroyed a pastoral way of life by
killing people and looting cattle. The Razaygqat and Baggara
are Muslim Arab tribes who were armed by the government
of Sudan to destroy the livelihood of Dinka people. Even
though the two peoples were historically neighbors, the
government armed and supported them to kill, destroy or
loot all things of Dinka. Armed with hatred and guns,
this was a holistic annihilation of the Dinka population by
Razayqat and Baggara tribes.

Khartoum targeted Dinka cattle to cripple the society.
Without cattle, Dinka could not pay dowries for marriage
or perform sacrifices for their ancestors. While cattle
cemented the bond between families in a Dinka marriage,

they also bring peace between the living and the dead in sacrifice. Everything from basic nutrition to prestige in the community came from cattle. The more you had, the more you were respected and considered rich or wealthy.

Thus, cattle posed obstacles to the spread of political Islam among the Dinka and other cattle-rearing tribes. So long as Dinka had plenty of cattle, they could not be bribed into abandoning their religions and culture. Tribes like Dinka, Nuer and others who depended on cattle were and still proud and resisted anything that challenges their cultures. In Dinka culture, cattle are used for sacrifices and spiritual reunion as well as Cattle cementing marriages, sacrifices and offered for family reunions. The following paragraphs illustrate roles that cattle play in Dinka culture.

In December, 2012, my wife and I took our children to Mayen Abun, South Sudan, for the first time. We were welcomed by my mother, my in-laws, and their relatives.

Two bulls were slaughtered to welcome us, and third one was sacrificed to my father.

When my mother sacrificed a bull for my father, I had to leave Mayen Abun around 3:00 a.m. and walk to Agok Adiang to be by my father's grave at the time of the offering. This was to thank my father for protecting us all along, especially in dangerous situations, and to unite my family with the spirit of my father. I asked my father for continued blessings.

Dinka slaughter bulls and goats for important guests. Dinka invoke the spirit of their totem by offering sacrifices for protection from sickness or evil spirits. They sacrifice bulls or goats for ancestors' spirits, especially when forgiveness is needed. Sickness and other problems require offerings to appease the anger of the gods, who are offended by the acts of the living. In addition to milk and meat that cattle provide to Dinka people, one's status in the society is decided by the number of cattle one has. Cattle are paid as the bride-price, so the more cattle one has, the wealthier he is. These were some of the reasons Dinka were targeted at the beginning of the civil war.

Khartoum rallied other tribes in South Sudan to support the government and fight against the rebellion, which were predominantly Dinka and Nuer. Dinka people were thought to be hard to please because they had cattle, so taking away their cattle would also rob them of their wealth and pride and bring them to submission. Dinka people were targeted by the government in Khartoum because the bulk of rebel soldiers, and their leader Dr. John Garang, were from Dinka tribe. The Khartoum regime tried to recruit South Sudanese from other tribes to join its militias and fight against the movement. Tragically, Dinka, as a tribe, was viewed as a sea where the SPLM/A movement could swim and draw support.

Genocide was unleashed against the Dinka, Nuer, and all the Southern ethnic groups, people of the Nuba Mountains, people of the Blue Nile, and all marginalized groups. The world had little to say about the tragedy that was unfolding in my country, whether from ignorance or from turning a blind eye. Nevertheless, the spirit of the oppressed South Sudanese could not be broken. We were determined to survive and to achieve total independence.

Desperate to survive, Dinka mothers had little choice left, so they "sold" their children for $300 to Razayqat buyers to obtain food for the remaining family members. These mothers were deceived into believing that they might get their children back. Some may have known that their children would never return, but the fact that these children would live and bring needed cash in for the survival of their family comforted them. Slavery was a tactic used to terrorize non-combatants into fleeing their territory. The abduction of Dinka women and children into slavery was a cultural and religious genocide that continued into the twenty-first century with no intervention from the rest of the world.

When Arab militias destroyed the village, our childhood rights and privileges were cut short. The tragedy of war sped up our growth. Children in many areas of South Sudan became adults before their time. Many children were forced to take up adult responsibilities and support their immediate family members who were left behind by the adults either killed or joined the SPLM/A. Children as young as fifteen years old took up adult responsibilities.

Although I was born in Mayen Abun, I grew up in Agok Adiang, where I enjoyed my childhood until the second civil war began in 1983 and changed things drastically. From his experience in the first civil war, my father advised me that war is evil and spares no one. Women and children were lumped in with rebel armies for Khartoum to destroy. No one recovers from the types of wounds that were inflicted in this war. Future generations were killed before they could grow to maturity.

When my village of Agok Adiang was destroyed, it seemed the whole world was on fire. The first time the Arab militia destroyed the village was around 1984. Those lucky to be alive scattered from the village in all directions. Some joined the revolution; others sought refuge; the rest went to

Northern Sudan. Many of these young boys and girls got to go to school. We realized that our possessions did not matter, and that we would have to make our own way in life based on our ability and mutual good will. When there is nothing left to stand on, or to begin with, one is forced by circumstance to navigate one's own destiny. When there are no shoulders to stand on, one must find one's own hilltops on which to stand.

Children in Twic had to fend for themselves because the government was targeting them instead of providing basic services such as: protection, education, clean water, and healthcare. There were few choices for children like me. I had to choose between joining the movement as a child and going north to face the wrath of my government. I chose to go North to see what I could find. I was lucky and had the opportunity to go to school.

The civil war in Sudan aimed not only to destroy rebels and southern intellectuals, but to wipe out the Dinka tribe and other ethnic groups that supported the SPLM/A. Government forces killed everyone, regardless of gender or age. Children were killed to extinguish future generations and to wipe out a culture. The fact that the South Sudanese waged a second war after AnyNya 1 was perceived by Khartoum as a failure of previous regimes. The wholesale killing is well documented. "It was indiscriminate slaughter, and acts of rapacity, little short of genocide, were rationalized by the need to destroy the SPLA's base," asserted Millard Burr and Robert Collins, who wrote a book about the tragic war ten years before the longest African civil war was resolved. [5]

The aim of the Sudanese government that recruited tribal militia was to make sure that the Dinka were scattered because the SPLA would be deprived of the supports from Dinka villages. This made the Dinka tribe the main target of the mass merciless killings. In both civil wars, the government was an enemy of its citizens.

The government of Sudan was committing genocide, yet the international community largely stayed silent or unaware of our ongoing murder. No media outlet covered the destruction of my village for the rest of the world to see. The tragedy unfolding in the Sudan was seen by our own eyes but by few others. We were attacked by our government and ignored by the rest of the world. No one came to our aid.

Governments that came and went in Khartoum targeted all sorts of resources in the South, which changed the pattern and operation of the war. In Southern areas like Twic, militias drove people away from their settlements by burning down houses, destroying crops, looting and slaughtering cattle, and abducting women and children into slavery.

After militias raided my village several times, leaving death and destruction in their wake, I had no choice but to leave. Like many young boys from my village, I had to

---

[5] J. Millard Burr and Robert O. Collins. Requiem for the Sudan: War, Drought, & Disaster Relief on the Nile. 1995, p. 19

start from scratch. I realized that there were chances out there for a better life, but I did not realize what hardships I would have to face to reach that better life. Most South Sudanese could not find opportunities to utilize their skill sets or potential to the fullest.

Our traditional way of life was blessed with many things that modern cities lack. Farming, fishing and hunting are still conducted with traditional tools and demand hard work for little yield. You find people using modern cell phones and internet, yet the majority still live in huts made of grass and mud. These people are part pastoralists and part farmers.

Most homes in Twic State were and are still made of grass-thatched huts with mud walls and wooden poles. Twic County, like many areas in southern Sudan, was subjected to decades of neglect, war, famine, and constant government persecution by various regimes in Khartoum. The governments that came and went made sure that the south was kept underdeveloped to prevent economic and political competition with the north.

People of Agok Adiang and other Twic were small farmers and cattle herders who depended on agriculture to live. The crops were never enough, so people subsidized their livelihood with hunting and fishing. Groups, using spears, hunted wild game. My uncle, Mabong Atem, was a great hunter. This need for group food gathering created cohesion and solidarity among the villagers. My uncle never returned home empty-handed after a group hunting or fishing trip. He always came home with fish and wild meat. If my uncle

Mabong was born in a country that provided opportunities, he would have been a world champion in running. He once caught a live deer. As it is, Uncle Mabong's talent will never be recognized.

People always shared any meat, even if it was not enough. Communal sharing was intact. The survival of the village depended on the solidarity of the men and women within it. Hunting was mainly done by men, while women fished. Like hunting for wild meat, fishing was also a communal activity. However, whereas hunters shared the meat, fishing gamers kept what they caught.

Because our actual ages were never known, boys decided their ages through fighting. You had to be tough to be respected by your peers. Younger boys would challenge older ones to try to beat the crap out of them! Sometimes fights were triggered by someone telling you or others that you are of the same age, or by someone claiming they are older than you when that is not the case.

When the second Sudanese civil war began, it became clear to the people of Twic County that destruction was inevitable. Able-bodied people had two choices: go north and risk enslavement, or go to Ethiopia to join the movement, and face hunger and wild animals. Boys and men lucky enough to be alive and not taken into slavery were expected to join the Sudan Peoples' Liberation Army/Movement. They went to Ethiopia to train at the rebels' base. By destroying Dinka villages and livelihoods, the Sudanese government and their allied militias also destroyed Dinka culture and values. Twic was one of many Dinka areas that recruited and supported the movement against Sudan's government.

Although my father believed in education, he did not want to send me far away from him, since he knew he was going to die from the wounds from war. It was not a matter of if but of when. My father decided to teach me how to run and manage our small family's business, since there was no school in Agok Adiang. Working at that small business, I used to sell tea. One day, it rained heavily, and I had to make tea in my maternal uncle's luak. A luak is bigger than a typical thatched hut. SPLM/A's soldiers came, drank my tea, and did not pay for the tea. These soldiers also took my cups! I had no choice but to follow them. I said to myself that if I did not get my teacups back, I was going to join the movement. I could never afford to buy new cups, and the way to Abyei where one could buy things like teacups was dangerous, so that seemed to be the end of my business.

The following morning, the commander of the army asked what I was doing with them, and he was informed about my teacups. Then the commander called and asked me to pick out my teacups, with a warning that if I took any teacup that did not belong to me, I would be whipped for fifty lashes. I agreed and about seventy teacups were brought before me. I managed to get back 29 out of my 31 teacups. The commander asked who my father was, and when I told him my father's name, he laughed and said, "You are like your father." He went on to tell me many stories of war that he had shared alongside my father during the first civil war.

The peace accord signed by the rebel leadership and

government in Khartoum was not recognized by some soldiers, including my father. The commander regretted the death of my father and wondered whether he would have joined the new movement if he were alive. Then, sounding just like my father, the commander told me how their leaders in the first movement rushed into a peace deal with Khartoum, and the Addis Ababa Accord was considered a sellout by the Anynya 1 leadership.

Deng Athuai Biar advised me to go and get an education in the north because he believed that when the south is liberated, there will be a need for educated South Sudanese to manage their country. After the interruption of my post-secondary education, I was frustrated from having studied but having no papers to prove it. I went back to my birthplace with the intention of joining the movement, even though Athuai advised me against. I believed that I had enough education and that it was time to commence my struggle with the marginalized.

As it turned out, the commander chose two soldiers to escort me home in the morning, safely. He advised me to go to the North and get an education. "We are fighting Arabs, and when we get our freedom, we will need educated people, so go and get an education," he stressed. The two soldiers and I left in the morning and reached my village, Agok Adiang, in the evening. My feet were sore, bleeding, and swollen from my long and fast barefoot walk. A few months later, my village, Agok Adiang, was destroyed by militias sponsored and supported by the Sudanese government.

I wanted to join the rebels, too, but I remembered the

rebel commander's piece of advice and what my own father had told me about war. I decided to move north in search of security and a better life. The next time the Arab militia attacked my village and everyone scattered, I ran with some people heading north and four days later found myself in the region of Abyei with little water and food.

After the destruction of Twic County, most people from Twic villages decided to move North through Abyei. Abyei is a land of nine Ngok Dinka chiefdoms: Abior, Achaak, Achueng, Allei, Anyel, Bongo, Diil, Man-nyar and Maren. I went to Abyei not only because of the war but because some of my family members lived in Abyei. My grandfather's second wife with her children lived there. It was in Abyei that my grandfather gave my mother the protecting spiritual spear. Against the will of my grandmother, the second wife of my grandfather, I went inside Abyei and found myself a job selling bannock, "a local donut". In a couple of months, I began to sell water by donkey.

After some months, I travelled to Muglad, north of Abyei. My four friends and I moved to El Obeid. I moved to Kosti and then to Khartoum where I became more conscious of my African heritage. I began identifying myself as African. I wanted to reclaim my lifestyle based on cattle and the culture that was destroyed. However, I knew that there was nothing left for me in the village, so I decided to find something else. I realized that education was the better option to replace the looted cattle.

One of the things that I never discussed with my father is religion. Even though my father was the oldest son of his father the customs and cultures dictated that my uncle, Kunyjokdit, whose father was the oldest son of the first wife in the family of eight wives, qualified for the family sacrifices' slaughtering spear.

At least those who escaped the bondage of slavery saw working as housemaids as an improvement in their status. These menial jobs watered seeds of change and allowed us to attend evening schools. I embarked on my education through evening school in a very harsh and unfriendly environment. Through education, I encountered Christianity.

CHAPTER 4

CHRISTIANITY AND EDUCATION

"It is through education that a daughter of
a peasant can become a doctor, that a son
of a mineworker can become the head of
the mine, that a child of farm workers can
become the president of a great nation." [6]

Education widens my prospects. Thankfully, formal
education and Christianity broadened my worldview. At
young age, I identified myself with my clan of Payath
Ateem. As my knowledge grew, I identified myself with my
ethnic group, Dinka. As my horizons expanded further,
I recognized myself as Southern Sudanese and later as
Sudanese, then as a refugee, and now a South Sudanese-
Canadian. All of these journeys were possible because of the
education that I acquired later on in life.

When South Sudanese went to Northern Sudan,
Christianity became their refuge. Christianity became a
symbol of resistance against the forced political Islamization.
The Sudanese government became adamant, and tried all
possible means to force South Sudanese into political Islam.
South Sudan rejected the religion that they identified with a

---

[6] Mandela, Nelson. Long Walk to Freedom 1995, (p. 32).

government that mistreated them. The number of Christians in the country grew tremendously. The Catholic Church in the north established and run many schools, most of which were in Khartoum, which is home to the majority of internally displaced persons within Sudan's borders.

As a teenager, I abandoned my African traditional religion to become a member of the Roman Catholic faith. In accepting Catholicism, I abandoned my African name, Atem, and chose a name of a Catholic saint, Martino, to be allowed baptism. With the sprinkling of water on my head, I changed my African religion and became a Roman Catholic believer. In my quest to belong to a strong and powerful religion, I threw away my heritage. I don't know what to tell my father when the time comes to meet him in the world of my ancestors, despite my comfort in Catholicism.

The foundation of my education was provided by schools established by the Roman Catholic Diocese of Khartoum. Seven years in the seminary have shaped my values.

After constant militia raids of cattle and killing of people of Twic County, I went in search of safety in Northern Sudan. While in Northern Sudan, I had the opportunity to work and attend evening schools. I realized I could get an education. There was some stability in the North, so most South Sudanese who went there for safety, especially the young boys, had the opportunity to pursue education. Most of these boys were doing menial jobs. Like many Southern Sudanese in the North, I jumped at the chance to get the education that I had had no access to while still in southern Sudan.

Like thousands of Twic Mayardit youths at the time, I had to create my own destiny. I embarked on a journey of education not because I thought I would go to college/university or go beyond an elementary education, but because I wanted to learn how to write and read my name. I grew up knowing few people who could read and write, and the idea that I could do so impressed me.

In the North, I had the opportunity to go to school and quench my desire for education. When I had the chance to go to school, I acted on the advice of the general who knew my father from the first civil war. He told me to go to Northern Sudan and get an education because the revolution, according to him, will need educated South Sudanese when the objectives are achieved and South Sudan becomes an independent entity.

My journey to education was an unplanned journey with lots of ups and downs. After sixteen or seventeen years of age with no hope of a formal education, I now participate fully in our Canadian society. I can communicate freely with people from all over the world. Thanks to Canadians and people of good will who have supported me to be what I am today: with their support, I was enabled, not only to graduate from university, but also to become a writer.

I could neither read nor write when I began working as a domestic worker in the town of Muglad, around 1986. After about a month of cleaning the house and washing clothes, I was promoted to selling ligamad, or "bannocks" in English. Ligamad is a famous sort of donut in Sudan, usually sold amongst children or eaten with tea.

I did housework in the early morning, and at about 7:00 a.m. each day I would go into the city to sell our local donuts. I was happy with the promotion, because selling ligamad helped me to find other boys from my village. Some had escaped from their slave-masters, and others had come to Muglad, like me, from Abyei. Three boys from my village and I planned to go further north to a city called El Obeid. El Obeid was the capital of the province of Kordofan at the time, and was bigger than Muglad.

At this time, the second Sudanese civil war was three years old, and thousands of people from the south had perished. To my friends and I, the war was waged by Dinka to liberate themselves from Arab domination. Our perspective was limited to knowledge of Dinka and Arabs. From the perspective of Agok Adiang and neighboring villages, our political and worldview was very limited.

Three of us decided to look for jobs in El Obeid. The only job we sought after was housework, since that did not require educational skills. Working in an Arab house was the most humiliating experience for Dinka boys, but it was the most available job and its only requirement was strength. Boys who escaped slavery, or managed to reach Northern Sudan safely, had nowhere else to go, so they turned to Arab families to work for food, water, and shelter, as well as protection from their former slave-masters.

In El Obeid, I found my maternal uncle who got me a job as a domestic worker in an Arab house, doing all of the housework. Looking back, I realize that the work I did was similar to the work of slaves in the past. Nonetheless, I

43

told the woman I worked for that I wanted to go to evening school, and that if she said no, I would leave her house. She accepted and told me not to inform my uncle about it.

I was very glad that my boss allowed it, and I began to attend a Comboni school in the evening. I also converted to Catholicism. When I began evening classes, I learned the Arabic language first, because that is what was taught by Comboni schools, which were run by Roman Catholic churches. Later on, as Islam and Arabic culture began to dominate the political and economic landscape of Sudan, Christianity became a unifying force for South Sudanese.

My uncle had no schooling, like most South Sudanese of his time, and did not value education, or at least not for me. I was too old to pass at any level, he believed; and because he opposed it, I decided to go further north to a city named Kosti. The woman I worked for in El Obeid dishonored our agreement and delayed me with lots of work whenever it was time for school, so I decided to go to Kosti without informing her or my uncle.

In Kosti, it did not take long to find a job, since all I needed was physical strength. Washing clothes, cleaning houses, and doing other menial jobs did not require an education. I found work with an East Indian family instead of an Arab one. This family allowed me to go to school in the evening. In fact, the owner of the house encouraged me.

"East Indian" is a term I learned in North America. This is to differentiate Indians from India and Indigenous people in Canada; the terminology is a relic from the time when all tribes in Canada were called Indians by the western colonizers.

My education is a product of the support that I have received from numerous people. Abraham Atem Aguer is among the people that assisted me in many ways. Aguer's firm support enabled me to pursue my education. Aguer's unweaving assistance from the beginning of my education to my time at St. Augustine's Minor Seminary in Khartoum, St. Paul's National Seminary (in both Philosophy and Theology at Kober-Khartoum Sudan), and finally to the Bahr El Ghazal University Faculty of Education in Wau.

I have confidence that with education, one can shape his/her destiny. I was sure that hard work would get me the education I needed, but was unsure where that education would take me. With education, I understood that South Sudanese were supposed to be equal citizens, and I began to understand what the war in the South was all about.

Peer pressure was a big challenge I faced as I was going to evening classes at a matured age. Many of my close friends and relatives told me I was wasting time by going to school. Some went as far as saying that evening education would never take me anywhere. These comments were daily occurrences, especially when I used the light of a relative's restaurant to study because there was no light at home.

Despite my investment in my studies, I never thought that one day I would sit and write something for other people to read. Atem Aguer supported and influenced me. He was my godfather when I was baptized in Kosti in 1987. In receiving a sprinkle of water on my head, I embraced Catholicism. In African religions, we prayed for all members of the family without a notion of heaven and hell. In Christianity, one's actions lead one to heaven or to hell, while in African religion; we worry about one another here and now.

Evening schools in Kosti, like in many places in the North, were meant to impart Catholicism. Abraham Atem Aguer was my mentor within Christianity. He helped me register in the evening school. Uncle Atem, as I call him, was a very strong supporter of my education. Abraham Atem Aguer supported my education in every way he could, even teaching me how to read and write the English alphabets. When the rest of my relatives in Kosti objected to my going to Khartoum, he insisted that I should go. Because other clan members in Khartoum had left school to join gangs and fight each other, my relatives feared that I would do the same, but Abraham Atem Aguer believed in my desire to get formal education.

At the bus station on March 23rd, 1988, in Kosti on my way to Khartoum, Atem Aguer gave me a final piece of advice, saying, "I am sure that you are stronger than Khartoum, and you will pursue your dream." I held this statement very dear, because it meant I should not follow peers who refused to educate themselves. Aguer had more confidence in me than I had in myself. His statement is one of the reasons I stayed focused on my education. I knew it was possible to get an education despite the challenges along the way.

After I was baptized, halfway through grade two learning Arabic and mathematics, I wanted to move somewhere that had better education and opportunities. I wanted to live where I could focus on my education without pressure from relatives or peers. The Indian family I worked for was so good that when they heard I wanted to further my education in Khartoum, they said I should go with them to Omdurman, Sudan's largest city, where I could study and work for their relatives. I accepted the opportunity.

Two days after my arrival in Omdurman, I again registered with the Catholic Church and the Comboni evening school. This time I registered in grade three even though I did not complete grade two in Kosti. Fortunately, no one bothered to ask for a school report card. These schools were meant to help adults learn basic things.

The school I was attending took place from 4:00 p.m. to 6:00 p.m., but it was not enough. I had time to attend another school from 6:00 p.m. to 8:00 p.m., so I registered in an Anglican evening school as well. I usually got to this school about fifteen minutes late every day, but the school administration was okay with it because I informed them in advance. In this school, I performed as well as in the other school. This education was an opportunity that I should have had when I was still young, but never did. I had a lot of catching up to do.

Daniel Comboni was a Roman Catholic bishop who went to Africa in 1857 and taught Christianity to Africans. Daniel Comboni is well-known by his motto: "Save Africa through Africa." After realizing that the African environment was not favorable to European missionaries, he trained Africans to preach Catholicism. In Sudan, Comboni missionaries worked as nuns and priests and they run schools for internally displaced people in Khartoum's outskirts. Most evening schools in Sudan tend to be called "Comboni schools," even when they have nothing to do with Catholicism. When I came to Khartoum, I realized how powerful these schools were. Most of those who did not have a chance to go to school in the South, when they were young, took advantage of these Comboni schools in the North. Most of the young men and women who went to these schools are now contributing to the nation-building of South Sudan at various levels of government of South Sudan.

In addition to evening schools, the archdiocese of Khartoum established morning schools for the internally displaced people in the North. After completing grade three in these two schools, I met an Italian nun by the name of Sister Lina, who worked as a missionary with the Comboni schools. After completing my housework one Friday, a public holiday in Sudan, I went to a Comboni school where I encountered groups of people studying the Bible. I asked if I could join them, and was welcomed by Sister Lina. I attended with this group, where people prayed after reading and discussing verses from the Holy Bible.

I became friends with Sister Lina. One day when we happened to be alone, we decided to talk about what I would do with my life instead of reading and discussing the Bible that day. From this discussion came the idea to go to seminary. I told her how eager I was to become a priest because the idea of helping people had occupied my mind since the floods of 1988 in Khartoum. Southern Sudanese suffered worse than anyone due to the occurrence of natural disasters, combined with lack of shelter, food, and clothing. With no time to waste, I told her that my problem was a lack of education, and she told me to do a placement test at the Khartoum North Sister Comboni School.

Although the sisters did not teach in this school, the sisters were the administrators, and so it was known as the sisters' school. It was 1989 when Sister Lina suggested that I do a placement test for grade six, which was quite a big gap from grade three. I skipped grades four and five, and sat for grade six. To my surprise, out of the seventy-odd students who took the test I had the top score! This result encouraged me greatly, and created in me a strong confidence that I could go even further with my education. When I first dreamed of school, I just wanted to write my name; now, I was realizing so much more.

After I completed grade six, Sister Lina asked me to apply to the seminary, which I did in 1990. Aguer encouraged me to go to seminary. When he realized that I did not have a pen or pencil, he gave me some blank papers as well as pencil. Stripped of my excuses, I wrote the exam and passed with flying colors. I began entry level classes in 1990, and was accepted to boarding seminary the following year. I attended St. Augustine's Minor Seminary for three years and spent one more year at a spiritual orientation in Khartoum. In Northern Sudan, I realized the disparity of wealth and development that existed between the South and the North.

I graduated from St. Paul's National Major Seminary in the philosophy section. Then, I attended St. Paul's National Major Seminary in the theology section. My decision to be a Roman Catholic priest was incompatible with Dinka tradition, which heavily relies on the importance of continuing the family line. Children among Dinka are seen as the ultimate achievement of humankind.

I was able to embrace the Catholic faith, but later on, I was too weak to resist my family's desire to continue the family lineage. The blood relations and family demands became thicker than the holy water that made me a Christian.

CHAPTER 5

BLOOD IS THICKER THAN HOLY WATER

Every Dinka fears dying without a son to "stand his head": to continue his name and revitalize his influence in this world.[7]

Celibacy is a foreign concept to Dinka tribe. In the dire situation that the Southern Sudanese were in, whether located in the south or in the north, we needed transcendent help. I sought God's guidance and inspiration in terms of what to do for myself and for those who needed more help than me. As mentioned in the previous chapter, a conversation I had with a nun during one of our weekly Bible studies inspired me to enter seminary to discern what I thought was God's call to priesthood. At the time, I had strong feeling that God was calling me to serve in the church as a priest. As I was approaching the altar of the Lord, the need to produce offspring to preserve our family line became stronger than the call to Catholic priesthood. Celibacy, which is necessary to become a Roman Catholic priest, does not exist in Dinka language. I gave in and accepted the voice of my family to continue with our family line.

---

[7] Deng, Francis Mading. The Dinka of the Sudan, 192, p. 9.

Even though my father went to the Congo during the first Sudan's civil war, he never told me about Christianity, or any other religion for that matter. I did not know about Christianity, so we never discussed any religion, despite the fact that my father and I spent much time together travelling. My father was preparing me to take over the family small business, since he knew his wounds were getting worse day by day.

I became interested in Christianity in El Obeid, where I started going to catechumen teaching. Before I received baptism, I had to take a name of a Catholic Saint, so, I chose Martino as my Christian name, a name that mother does not know even now. In the process, I abandoned Atamyath, and embraced Christianity, specifically, Catholicism.

My mother, family, relatives and my extended family considered my decision to become a Roman Catholic priest to be the end of my father's linage since I was my father's only son. In South Sudan, tribe, ethnicity, and region are seen as protective institutions. Celibacy was foreign to my family. Even worse, being my mother's only son made it unthinkable and unacceptable.

In 1996, when my maternal uncle, Deng Bulluk, known as Deng Awergook, came to Khartoum, he refused to meet me unless I left the idea of priesthood. Although I did not decide to leave the seminary then, I assured him that I would marry, because he did not know what seminary was. After a few minutes of conversation regarding family members back home, Deng Awergook told me that he was ready to spend any number of cattle to treat my disease. I began to laugh because he thought I did not want to marry because I was unable to produce offspring due to an illness.

My family members and relatives were not Christians. My entire families on both sides were animists. They have their own gods, yaath, which are symbolized by different totems. The Christian idea of someone not getting married because he wants to serve God did not make sense to them. When I was sure that my maternal uncle was now in a position to talk, I began to explain to him why I wanted to become a priest. I took the opportunity to persuade him so that he would, in turn, convince my mother, his step-sister. Nevertheless, this strategy was ineffective. Uncle Deng Awergook was not moved at all. Awergook looked at me surprised that I would continue with what seemed like nonsense to him.

My maternal uncle ignored my persuasion to become a priest and, instead turning to the people who were present in the house. He laughingly said, "What kind of Nhialic [i.e., God] wants people to serve him by not getting married?" I became a laughing stock for the people present. My maternal uncle, who was named Kuot, after Kuonyath, laughed for about fifteen minutes, teasing me and my new Nhialic. He said, "Is this the white man's God?" I responded no, it is not the white man's God, but God for everyone." Before I could continue, a lady who was present interrupted me and said, "These white people have their children and when they become old, they come to Africa to control us, telling lies." She pointed at me, saying, "Boy, if you are responsible, just be sincere and stop beating around the bush. What kind of God prevents people from getting married?"

When I was able to respond to this lady, my maternal uncle Manut Bulluk interrupted me and said, "If that is the God you are studying in school, your school is useless." He continued, "You'd better go back to Southern Sudan and help your mother and your sisters because a Dinka's wealth is mainly measured by the number of cattle and children one has. Death never stops a Dinka man demands having his lineage preserved. As time went on and learned more about my culture, realized that my father would not support the idea of my becoming a Roman Catholic priest.

Every attempt I made to try to have a meaningful conversation with them about Jesus Christ was in vain. I turned to my cousin, Majak Atem Maktung (whose Christian name is Joackino, derived from Joachim, father of the Virgin Mary, the mother of Jesus). I once questioned Majak why he chose the name Joackino, instead of Jochim, but he asked why I chose Martino instead of Martin. I did not have an answer, so we respected the other's choice. (I had previously persuaded Joackino to join St. Augustine's Minor seminary in Khartoum. He studied there for about two and half years, but he eventually left seminary saying God does not want bribe. When I asked what he meant by bribe, Joakino said, "Why do I have to sacrifice the lineage of my family to please God?" Joackino is weir sometimes but he got his way to argue his point. I told him becoming a priest is not bribing God but follow the footsteps of Jesus who did not marry. He said, "My friend Jesus had both human and divine natures while we humans have one nature

Joackino and I together left Abyei for Muglad. Then, we went to El Obeid where he met my maternal uncle, Manut Bulluk, and became his close friend. Uncle Manut sometimes drank alcohol with Joackino, and the two became friends. I wanted Joackino to use that good relationship to help me out.

Joackino is very smart, and I knew he could come to my defense if he chose to. Realizing that I was expecting his support, Joackino started relaying stories from the Bible, saying, "Jesus Christ is a real Son of God." He added, "One of the things I like about Jesus is that his first miracle was turning water into wine." People were drinking as Joackino told the story, so it was a good point at the time. Joackino continued, "Jesus is like Atamyath Wa, in that he does not prevent people from drinking alcohol like figures of other religions," Joackino was referring to Islam. He continued, "In fact, during harvest, we offer Atamyath wine." People laughed. He said, "The only problem I have with Christians is the fact that they believe that God has power to take human nature in the form of Jesus Christ, but they do not think that the same God has the power to accept our prayers through Atamyath as well as his mother Arou." Arou ("tortoise") is the mother of Atamyath according to Payathatam belief.

Clever as he was, Joackino realized that the majority presence in the house were my maternal uncles from Pagour. Pagour is the clan of my mother and so most people in the discussion were from my mother's side. Joackino asserted, "Kuonyath, your yath does not prevent people from drinking alcohol." He pointed to my maternal uncles who believe that Kuonyath, their god, intercedes for them in times of needs. Kuonyath is symbolized by pumpkin or lion.

Joackino turned to me and said, "My friend, I have told you many times to leave that seminary." He asserted, "The vocation of Catholic priesthood is not meant for Dinka people. This notion of man dying without wife, wives or children is against our culture", Joackino emphasized. Joackino called me my friend even though we are extended cousins. He looked into my eyes and said, "My friend, take this beautiful wife of your maternal uncle and give her children. If do not, your late maternal uncle will curse your ass". He turned to my later uncle's wife and said, "If Atem does not want you because of his "God" I will be happy to produce children with you for your late husband." Everyone present, including Joackino, knew very well that she could not be given to him because he is not related to my late maternal uncle. My maternal uncle, Deng Awergook, gave Joackino a drink.

My late uncle's wife who had been silent all these time took Joackino's statement as an invitation to the discussion. She joined the conversation and told those sitting that she wanted to know why I refused to have children with her for my late uncle. Everybody jumped on me and supported my maternal wife.

Since I declared in their presence that I had abandoned my desire to follow my new Nhialic, the issue of priesthood was made irrelevant. I told them that since I was the first-born of my father and our totem, Atemyath would never allow me to have children for my maternal family before I bore my own children for our family. It is a belief that any first born male in my clan must bear children that belong to Payathatem before he procreates children into his maternal family. My uncle Deng Awergook responded saying he would pay a bull to Atamyath. I tried my level best to reject, but without any success.

So I called my uncle's wife to a private rakuba, a room made out of pieces of broken vehicles and sacks, and told her I would accept her only if she let me go back to seminary. I also wanted her to go to Southern Sudan, and I would follow after three months when the school closed for the year. She accepted with a doubt in her mind. After this discussion with my mother and other relatives, I realized I was swimming against strong and undefeatable waves. I abandoned my desire for religious life in the priesthood. I surrendered to the family demand and realized that family blood relations were thicker than the holy water that I was baptized with into Catholicism.

Everyone in the meeting began preaching to me about why it is important for me to produce children for my late uncle. My maternal uncle, Kuot Malou, left behind three wives, but one left him while he was still alive, so one of the remaining wives wanted me to produce children for my late maternal uncle. She was more persuasive than anyone else in the room. After a long discussion, I gave in.

My late uncle's wife Nyanut, immediately stated that

she wanted to talk with me alone about how my mind had changed. She wanted to know whether I accepted my traditional obligation of taking her or whether I had just agreed to please my maternal uncles in the meeting. We started talking; our conversation lasted for many hours. She had the last word, and she told me that she would wait for me for a few months, but that if I did not show up in Twic in two to three months, she would have to find someone related to the family. I agreed.

Dinka people value children more than anything else. One of the reasons for having many children was and still among the Dinka, is that a man's legacy is measured by the number of children he has or left behind. Another reason for more children was to fill the need for manpower to cultivate farms and provide hard labour, which was necessary since the tools used were technically less developed. In addition to these reasons, the infant mortality rate was high due to the lack of medical facilities.

People of Twic State, like many Dinka sections, practice both polygamy and ghost marriage. Both marriages are unique to Dinka and a few similar tribes in South Sudan. The supporters of ghost marriage argue that the rights of the dead are respected through a continuation of the dead man's right. This is one of the reasons that ghost marriage is prevalent among the Dinka people of South Sudan.

In the old days, polygamy among the Dinka was valued to the point that a man with one wife was considered to be poor and sometimes irresponsible. Dinka marriage is costly to the groom, because he and his family members, relatives, and friends have to pay the bride-price to the bride's family. So having more wives requires a great deal of wealth from the groom. Since polygamy has been practiced for many decades, Dinka people have made into a culture and it is simply the practice nowadays.

In Dinka culture, polygamy is one of the ways to produce more children and acquire social prestige. Polygamy is one of the oldest cultures that Dinka people have been practicing for centuries. Some Dinka politicians and chiefs, exclusively the beneficiaries of polygamy, argue that polygamy is one of the reasons why Dinka is the largest ethnic group in the Republic of South Sudan. Polygamy becomes a factory for children.

In addition to the practice of polygamy, a male whose younger brother dies before being married will marry a wife for his deceased brother. This is what anthropologists call ghost marriage. Ghost marriage has existed among the Dinka people for a very long time. The strength of this custom is hard to abandon. It is considered moral obligation for younger male to marry a girl for his late brother who had died before he got married. If a male dies leaving behind a wife or wives, his brother or sons of his sister will continue to procreate for him. So, my maternal family was asking me to carry out my cultural responsibility. In Dinka, death does not prevent a man from having children because children surpass all things.

Failing to procreate in Dinka was unheard of, and it amounted to violation of one of Dinka's fundamental values, *koc e nhom.* This value in Dinka society explains why polygamy is still so prevalent. To be respected by the Dinka, men must marry and produce many descendants. In my section of Twic Mayardit Dinka, when people hear that a man has died, they ask whether he died fully or half dead. If the deceased bore children in life, he is half dead, but if he bore no children, then he has died fully. As a Dinka man, I have to go against some Dinka fundamentals. Dinka people believe that man's status is determined in terms of number of wives and children he has.

One of the main reasons I attended seminary was to serve Christians who were mistreated in Northern Sudan. Christians and African traditional religions' believers living in Northern Sudan were constantly living in fear of their Northern brothers. I did encounter threats in Southern Sudan from Arab militias and also in the North. Moreover, when I came to Southern Sudan, I faced threatening moments when I was confronted by armed Southern Sudanese.

I decided to quit seminary, and then joined Bahr El Ghazal University located in the town of Wau, in Southern Sudan. Had I continued in seminary and become a priest, I don't know what my father in the world of the dead would have thought of me.

CHAPTER 6

UNPLEASANT SITUATIONS

We fought injustice wherever we found
it, no matter how large, or how small,
we fought injustice to preserve our own
humanity. [8]

Unpleasant situations strengthened my determination.
When police officers put me in their truck, I thought they
would take me to a police station and would then release me.
After all, I had not done anything wrong. However, after a
few minutes in the truck, the whole scenario turned out to
be a threat on my life. I had taken an active role in telling
the world what the Sudanese government was doing to our
people in camps for internally displaced people. This choice
was risky, because if the police force were to discover what
I was doing, I would have been imprisoned and charged
with treachery. The many threats on my life were setbacks
and tests of my faith in humanity. Unfortunately, such
experiences were common among children growing up in
the Sudan at the time.

In 1988, I heard that my sisters were in El Obeid with
our maternal uncle, Manut Bulluk, so I went to bring them

---

[8] Mandela, Nelson. Long Walk to Freedom 1995, p. (406)

to Khartoum to live with me. On my way to El Obeid, I stopped to spend the night with friends and relatives who lived in Jaraf Gharab, part of western Khartoum.

My encounter with police in Jaraf Gharab was an eye opening experience that I will never forget. It taught me that Arab Muslim elites betrayed Islam and Arabs. I stopped to chat with Southern Sudanese friends who were selling cigarettes at the bus station, like many of our youth did. That form of income was discouraged by the government, so a police truck came to pick up the cigarette sellers. I was just talking with friends, so I felt no need to run like the others who had been selling cigarettes when the police began chasing.

These young men were selling cigarettes because it was their only way of earning a living. These young men from South Sudan were not included as full members of their country. They were barred from the key economic, social, and political activities required growing and participating in life and society. They were denied participation in basic economic, social, and political activities in their own country. Nevertheless, their struggle to survive selling cigarettes became their crime.

When the police truck came, the young men who had been selling cigarettes ran as fast as their legs could carry them. I refused to run like the rest, because I knew I had done nothing wrong. However, I was caught and put onto the police pickup truck. I was kicked and hit with a gun a couple times. One officer began suggesting that a bullet could not kill me. He compared me to a person who had shot and killed some members of organized forces the previous night. In that police truck, I feared for my dear life.

One police officer asked me if it was true that a bullet could not kill me. It was difficult to answer such a question, but I quickly responded that I knew nothing about the man they were talking about. I then replied, "Yes, a bullet could kill me." Death was so near that I did not know whether I would live or die. One officer suggested shooting me, but a more sensible officer replied, "Are you crazy? How you can shoot him in the truck? If you want, we can take him to a faraway place; then, we will kill him and leave him over there."

I was really scared, but there was nothing I could do. I just kept praying. I prayed first to my father, and then to Jesus. I had to pray quietly, because exposing my religions, Dinka and Roman Catholicism, would make things worse. I prayed silently, worried about the money I had on me more than I worried about my death. I was blaming myself for not giving the money to my cousin, Abraham Atem, who would have sent it to my sisters in El Obeid if I died there. It was supposed to be transportation money for myself and my sisters.

My mind turned away from fear, and I began to think about the nature of death. I did not want to be slaughtered as a sacrificial lamb. I started to blame Deng Biar, who had talked me out of joining the revolution. At least there would be a possibility that I could have killed someone in defense of my people and my country. If I were to die fighting, my death would have been an honor to my people and my country. I started remembering all those people who were killed fighting for freedom. I thought to myself, if I were to be killed in a war, South Sudanese history would remember me among the country's freedom fighters.

Facing death, those who entered my mind were the ones who had fought for our freedom. They were fighting to liberate South Sudan. I was no longer afraid to die — but how would it happen? To die fighting the Sudanese government or their sponsored militias would have been better than dying this way.

If I were to die fighting, my name would be added to the list of martyrs who died liberating their people. Dying for South Sudan was an honor that my father in his grave would appreciate. My father would proudly welcome me to the world of death, if I were to die fighting the war that he and his colleagues left unfinished.

At that time in Khartoum, all Southerners were considered rebels or rebel sympathizers, especially the Dinka. After all, the leader of the SPLM/A, Dr. John Garang, was a Dinka. The government of Sudan labeled the rebellion a Dinka movement to discourage the other sixty-three ethnic groups of Sudan from joining the revolution.

While in the police pickup truck, my thoughts were with my sisters who I had not seen for a long time, as well as with my mother. The world was coming to an end for me, slowly but surely, I thought to myself. I wished again that I had a chance to give the money to Abraham Atem. Without a doubt, he would have sent that money to my sisters. I worried that these "devil soldiers" would benefit from the money I had worked hard for. I wanted it all to be a dream, but every second in the truck was all too real.

Hope became a reality when the truck stopped at the station and the commanding police officer came over and saw me sitting in the truck. He asked me what I had been selling at the station, but before I could reply, an officer told him that I had been selling nothing and that I was being threatened by the other officers. This officer defended me to the point that I said nothing. I could not believe what I was hearing. He reprimanded the officers.

I felt my life was in the hands of that captain and that he would have ended it if he'd chosen to, but he proved to me that not everyone in uniform in Sudan was evil. The commanding officer surprisingly told me to get out of the truck and wait by the shop nearby for a bus to take me home. He asked me if I had money for bus fare. I responded, "Yes," immediately. I could not believe my ears. I instantly jumped out of the truck and ran! The officers in the truck laughed as I sped away from the pickup truck. I began to thank my father and then Jesus. I was not sure who intervened first, but I received the help I needed.

On my way home, I met my cousin Atem Makilkil, who was going to a police station to file a report about my case. Makilkil was glad when he saw me from far away, and we went home, where we found Abraham Atem in bed crying because he did not know whether I would return or not. Abraham Atem Aguer got up with joy with he saw us. But it was not the last time I would be threatened.

Another unpleasant incident happened when the director of seminary and I went to one of the displaced persons camp in Khartoum.

In 1993, the Sudanese government decided to take all internally displaced persons (IDPs) to a desert and settled them there. These internally displaced persons (IDPs) were mostly from marginalized areas of South Sudan, including the Nuba Mountains and the Blue Nile areas. The IDPs faced enormous challenges where they were settled. The government named the settlement Madina Salam, meaning "peace town," but the people, taken there by force, called it "Jaborana," which in Arabic loosely means, "We are forced."

These people had no choice but to accept the forced relocations. The government did not like the name Jabarona, and so people were forbidden to use it. The government punished those who used the name until they realized it could never succeed. As the saying goes, "Where there is a will, there is a way." These marginalized people refused to call the place "peace town," knowing they had never been consulted, nor had they been given the choice to refrain from relocating. In addition to the forced nature of the relocation, these people now had no food, shelter, or water.

International NGOs were not allowed to operate in these desert camps. Only Islamic organizations such as Dawa were allowed entry to provide food aid. These organizations forced people to embrace Islam as a requirement to receive food.

The most targeted people were young children, who were

told to profess Islam by simply saying the Shahada. Reciting Shahada implies accepting and professing of Islamic faith. Shahada goes, "There is no God but Allah, and Muhammad is his Prophet." This was the first condition for children to receive food, and since many of these children had no parents to provide for them, they quickly converted to Islam. The second condition was to attend the Qur'anic schools in Jabarona and other camps where IDPs were staying.

The conditions in these camps were horrible and inhumane, but these internally displaced persons had no choice. The women resorted to brewing local wine as a source of income, which became a crime for thousands of women. Sudan's Islamic government applied Sharia law to anybody found drunk or selling alcohol, and violators were jailed and fined. Even after Sharia laws stopped being officially applied, the southern women suffered through arbitrary arrests.

The partial application of Sharia Law mostly affected marginalized women from Southern Sudan, the Nuba Mountains, and other areas affected by war and natural disasters. Many women, including those pregnant, spent time in jail because they could not afford to pay the fines. The application of Sharia Laws in June 1983 by the Sudan government was more motivated by politics than religion.

In Sudan, mostly men drank alcohol. The partial and undeclared implementation of Sharia law was that, if a person caught drinking or drunk, he would receive fifty (50) lashes for crime of drinking. One time a judge sentenced a man named John to 50 lashes and witnessed the punishment being administered. To his surprise, John asked for another 50 lashes. When the judge asked why, John said, "I will drink wine tomorrow and I don't want to come back here tomorrow." The judge laughed and said, "You will be fined for drinking wine tomorrow because we have arrested the women that brew wine in Jebel Aulia." The man responded, "I know how to do it, so I will do it myself." The judge said, "We will lash you tomorrow after we have evidence you were drinking." He dismissed the man.

When John was asked later about his motives, he said he wanted to show the judge that he was determined to never obey the laws of another faith.

The women received more punishments than men under Sharia law for brewing alcohol. Through brewing local alcohol, Areki business, women were the breadwinners for their families. Many women gave birth in prison. When I was a seminarian, I attended many masses in prison both for men and women. As a minor seminarian, I used to go with my parish priest to celebrate Eucharistic celebrations with the prisoners at Christmas and other Catholic holidays, even in my time off between semesters.

There are times and situations when you cannot stand aside and let your people suffer alone. I was sad I could not do more. Visiting and listening to the stories of these poor women motivated me to pursue the priestly vocation. At the time, I thought that was one possible way to assist them. I thought to myself that as a priest, I would be able to tell their stories to those who have power and willingness to help.

There was no doubt in my mind that these women had been abandoned by the international community.

I tried to help in any way I could, since I was not in the liberation army. I found someone with my same passion, if not greater, who had access to the international community. Father Edward Brady was an American Jesuit priest who was a spiritual director at St. Paul's National Major Seminary, Spiritual Orientation, in Khartoum.

One time I met Fr. Brady in one of my routine spiritual meetings, and I shared with him what was disturbing me: "the situation my people were living in". At that moment it seemed he was thinking along the same line, except that he had no access to the IDP camps. We immediately agreed on the roles each one of us would play. Fr. Brady assigned me to go and take pictures of the situation in camp and bring them to him. Fr. Brady, in turn, would send these pictures to some human rights groups. I was not aware which groups, but I was glad that the inhumane suffering of my people was getting out to the international community. I thought that the international community would pressure the Sudanese government to allow international non-profit organizations to the camp to provide for people's basic needs and would also put pressure on the warring parties to come to a political settlement.

I saw my collaboration with Fr. Brady as the one thing I could do to expose the evil that government of Sudan was subjecting my people to. The Sudanese government had all the obligations, legal and moral, to protect these people. Instead, the government became the actual source of the people's suffering. Their goal was to break the spirits of the displaced people and to make them weak enough to embrace Islam and its culture.

One day, I went to Jabarona with an Italian Roman Catholic priest, but because he did not have the required permit to enter the camp, we sent for a Sudanese Catholic priest to come and negotiate with the police. The Sudanese priest came and negotiated with the police to allow the Italian priest into the camp. While we were waiting for the priest, I hid the camera under my seat and sat in the car for more than an hour. I was afraid that if they discovered me taking pictures for outsiders, it would be the end of my life. We were allowed in the camp for one hour, and although I managed to take some pictures that day, I was absolutely scared to death.

I was lucky that the camp was meant for us Southerners, so they did not bother me. I was scared about the camera and my heart was pounding through my chest, but I took pictures to show the world the injustice happening in the outskirts of Khartoum. As I sat in the car waiting for the priest, I thought about all the people I knew in prison. What would be my fate if I was arrested? Would I even get out? When Rev. Father Michael Didi finally came, we were released and given an hour in the camp. This time restriction was actually meant for the Italian priest. As a Southerner, I had no problem staying in the camp as long as I wanted. As I learned more about SPLM/A's power struggle, there was no doubt that the greed for power in the SPLM/A's leadership would prolong the suffering of our people.

The power struggle within the SPLM/A ranks created many setbacks to the revolution. Major Kerubino, the man who shot the first bullet that sparked the second Sudan Civil War on May 16th, 1983, was imprisoned in 1987 on unfounded allegations of an attempted coup against the Commander-in-Chief Dr. John Garang. Kerubino was arrested with the support of Ethiopian security operatives and was imprisoned without trial for over five years.

In 1992, Major William Nyoun Bany, who replaced Kerubino, also feared being arrested. He deserted the movement and released all of high commanders who were detained without due process, including Kerubino, who was second in command in the leadership of the movement.

In April 1997, Kerubino and SPLM/A's high-ranking members signed a peace agreement with the Khartoum government. The Khartoum government, as usual, dishonored the agreement. When Kerubino realized this, he decided to go to the Bahr El Ghazal region in the south. The students at Bahr El Ghazal University were alarmed at the number of soldiers of the SPLM/A into Wau city. When Kerubino was stationed at Marial Baai, students from Bahr el Ghazal University and I decided to visit him. We had a hot and lengthy debate regarding who would be involved in the visit.

The debate was among the Dinka students at the university. It was finally decided that only Dinka students would go, and if Kerubino decided to kill them, let it be. Since Kerubino was Dinka, the Dinka students decided to challenge him on what appeared to be SPLM/A soldiers surrendering themselves to government forces in the city of Wau.

The students were bitter about the situation in Wau, which we felt was unacceptable. We wanted Kerubino to rejoin the SPLM/A, the movement that he spearheaded in 1983. The students set up a committee to visit him, which included three students from Twic Mayardit, Kerubino's home: Mangor Barac, Paulino Agai, and the author. Along with eight other students, we went to Marial Baai on January 11th, 1998. I was chosen to go and meet Kerubino for two main reasons. First, I was the Secretary of External Affairs for the South Sudanese Students' Union at Bahr El Ghazal University, and second, I was from Twic District, home of Gen. Kerubino.

When asked about supplying the students with arms, Kerubino answered that Khartoum was fully aware of his intentions of rejoining the SPLM/A. He said that the North and South had reached the point where no one could deceive the other. Kerubino and everyone there agreed that the divide between the North and the South had been drawn. When Kerubino explained why he was jailed and how he was treated, I saw the bitterness that my father had about his colleagues in the Anynya 1, whom my father believed betrayed, the cause of the people.

Khartoum was aware of Kerubino's plans to rejoin the movement, but the government did not want to provoke him. The government hoped to trick Kerubino into going back to Khartoum, where they could arrest or kill him, but Kerubino was not about to fall into their trap. After

Kerubino assured us, the students, of his plans a committee was formed.

Three students from the university were elected by the committee to supervise any relief supplies that students brought from Khartoum to Kerubino's forces at Marial Baai. General Kerubino tasked the committee to alert his forces about the regime's intention in sending these national aid items. The students who came from Khartoum had a political motive to bribe Southerners.

University students from all over Sudan, north and south, wanted to visit Kerubino in Marial Baai. There were three vehicles from our university and three other rented vehicles from students in Khartoum. According to the rules of the new committee that General Kerubino had set up earlier, some of our team members had to accompany any student group(s) visiting him in Marial Baai. This committee was to make sure that the soldiers would not forget the cause of the SPLM/A.

On one of the trips to Marial Baai, I was asked by the committee to accompany students from Khartoum. I was late to the pickup truck before leaving the city, and I found an Arab student from the Bahr El Ghazal University seated in the front passenger's seat. Since I was one of the high-ranking students' organization in the committee, I asked the student to come down and get in the back of the pickup truck.

The student first refused to get out of the front seat. I told him I would not go if he did not come down. "Up to you," the student responded. I told the driver I was not going, and when some girls from the Bahr El Ghazal University saw me outside the truck, they got out of their vehicle, too. The Arab student then got out and asked me to sit in the front seat, which I gladly accepted. The journey went smoothly, and though I appeared rude, I felt justified in doing what was needed in the context of the time. I wanted to send a clear message that we were in charge in Southern Sudan. I knew the student was an employee of the national security of Khartoum government.

As General Kerubino promised, the southern students at the Bahr El Ghazal University were informed early, on January 11th, 1998, of his forces' imminent attack on the government army. The day before the shooting erupted, Mangor and I went to friends and relatives looking for guns. We managed to secure one gun, which Mangor put under his "Jallabia," a long-sleeved garment. We concealed the gun under Mangor's Jallabia and brought it to the campus where we lived.

On our way to the campus, Mangor and I met some of General Kerubino's security personnel and asked them for updates. One of the men responded that there was nothing going on and that the students should not worry. He said he would inform us if there was anything happening, because he was from our home area of Twic. Mangor and I could not believe our ears, so we went home with the only gun we had secured.

On the evening of January 28th, 1998, an altercation took place between an Arab bakery owner and his employee, who happened to be a Dinka boy. The Dinka boy was verbally and physically abused by the owner. I was so upset that I wanted to fight since I did not know better at the time. However, Mangor Barac knew that the war would begin at night and that I would neither fight nor survive if I were in a government jail cell. Mangor advised me to control myself. Had I attacked the owner of the bakery, I would have received temporary cell time. I later learned that most Southerners in the prison cells from January 29–30 were murdered in cold blood. Thanks to Mangor for his wise advice.

The government of Sudan was worried about the situation in Marial Baai, where General Kerubino's forces were stationed. Because Khartoum feared Kerubino returning to the movement, the divide in Wau between southerners and northerners grew wider every day, inching closer to war. When the Dinka boy was beaten up at the bakery, it was because the Arab bakery owner considered himself superior to Dinka people and thought that the boy had no right to disagree with him. Sudanese Arab Muslims considered themselves superior to non-Arab, non-Muslims, which is an unsubstantiated belief.

After a long walk, Mangor, Atem and I joined the family of our Dean for the Faculty of Education at the Bahr El Ghazal University. We walked for another hour or so; then, we came to a tree and took a break. Mangor and I went off by ourselves for a few minutes. We were looking for something to eat, but our search was in vain. When we returned, we were met by SPLM/A soldiers who ordered us to put down the guns we received from soldiers. One soldier was shot, while the other soldier gave me his gun because he had to carry one of his children. Mangor wanted to refuse, but I told him we had to put them down.

We were in the middle of nowhere and the soldiers might kill us and leave at any time. I was scared, not knowing what the soldiers were up to and what they could be capable of. I began to remember the people who were killed in my village because they refused to obey "stupid orders". I was worried about what would happen next. Thank God, our former dean of our college paid money to these soldiers who then, let us go after they received the money. After these soldiers left us alone, we continued on our way to Nyang Akoc Majok. I had no idea where we were or how long we had to walk before reaching Nyang Akoc. We walked exhaustedly for seven or eight hours nonstop, with no food and just a little dirty water before we arrived at Nyang Akoc Majok.

I did not know how to fire a gun! I had a policeman's gun, which he gave me when he had to carry his own children. I surrendered it to the soldiers because I had never shot a gun in my life, a move which gave these well-trained soldiers the upper hand, I assumed. First, I persuaded Mangor to put down the guns we had because picking a fight with these soldiers was not a wise thing to do, so I begged Mangor to put down our guns. This incident opened my eyes to the reality of what SPLM/A soldiers could do. The fact that they did not have salaries of any sort manifested itself to how the treat others. Some SPLM/A soldiers never underwent any proper training in terms of the objectives of the movement and how they should treat civilians. The fact that they had guns meant to them they control everyone that had no gun.

Thirdly, whatever we did would have immense ramifications for the rest of the group. Our English lecturer at the Bahr El Ghazal University and his family were with us, as well as several other families we picked up along the way. Thank God that Mangor quickly understood and did not resist. After we put down the guns, one of the soldiers collected them and asked us to follow them to where our people were resting. Neither of us (Mangor nor the author) could negotiate with the soldiers who took our guns.

Well, they were not our guns, but we had them in our hands and so at that time they were ours. Mangor had a gun that belonged to Martin. Mr. Martin was shot while fighting in Wau town. As soon as Mangor, Atem and I left the residence on the campus, we saw one of the soldiers from our area Twic was bleeding from gunshot. Mangor knew him and he said, "Martin let's go." Martin, the wounded soldiers said, must revenge for his wound, but Mangor warned him of the grave consequences if he did not leave the city. Fortunately, Mr. Martin yielded to Mangor's advice and he left with us and since his bleeding was increasing, we found someone with bicycle who agreed to carry on his bicycle. So Martin gave his gun to Mangor.

We spent a whole day of walking going toward Nyang Akoc Majok, and at about 8:00 p.m., a wife of our teacher Lino was so fatigued from the walking that she fainted, so we lit a fire with wood from the forest we were in. Another group of soldiers came, and instead of feeling sympathy for the poor woman, they ordered Mangor and I to go back to the city of Wau with them. Lino pleaded for help, but it was in vain. They never listened, only saying that we were going back to Wau. Since all of our belongings were in Wau, we also wanted to go back, but not when our help was badly needed at that time.

The lady who fainted was not only our teacher's wife, but she was also Mangor's sister! We thought the soldiers were serious when they said they wanted us to go back to fight in Wau, but we found them to be liars. Once back, they went to every house they could and searched for food without asking the owners for permission. None of the men in these homes were allowed to talk to the soldiers, who took any food they laid their hands on. I heard that during the SPLM/A training, Dr. John Garang told his army graduates that their newly distributed Kalashnikovs were their mother, father, and even food. The soldier's gun was his provider, so to speak.

When the SPLM/A soldiers were in training, they were taught, "Do not take by force, but do not let go of" whatever it was they wanted. This meant they would beg but never let the person they begged to leave with the desired items. It was a known truth that when a soldier asked for something, you had to give it, because the soldier would take it no matter what.

My encounter with an SPLM/A soldier in Malual Ayuong was another example of how SPLM/A soldiers could treat their own people. I was coming from Madhol when I was asked by an SPLM/A officer who I was and where I was going. This was a common thing with the rebels. I told the officer my name, where I was from, and where I was going. Where you are from and where you are coming from were two different things for the SPLM/A. As it happened, the officer was from my birthplace, Mayen Abun. I was relieved to hear it, but when I told him that I was carrying rice, biscuits and sugar, he cried aloud that he had not tasted any of those items in a long time. The officer knew I would not leave without giving some of my food to him and his bodyguards.

The officer then asked a woman who was pounding sorghum to bring a gourd, so I could give him and his bodyguards some sugar, biscuits, and rice. I explained to him that I was carrying these things so that I could get my sick sister to a place where she could receive treatment. He did not believe me, so I told him bluntly that I refused to give him anything he wanted, and that he would need to use force to get it. Kerubino had prohibited taking things from civilians by force, and if I had let him take what he wanted, I would have reported it directly to Kerubino, in nearby Wunakec.

When I bluntly told the captain that I was not going to give him any food, he was surprised. According to a statement from Kerubino, looting was not allowed, and the officer was aware of this. I left, but did not use the path leading to Panyok. I was afraid that the bodyguards might follow me into the forest, where, all alone, they could do what they wanted and even kill me. I had to climb a tree to make sure I was not lost or being followed. I began to wonder what kind of a country we would have if we became independent. Another incident that made me feel threatened was when Paul invited Fr. William who asked me to accompany him to his headquarters at Pariack.

Paul was the commanding SPMA officer in Northern Bahr El Ghazal. On June 2nd, 1998, Fr. William and I were picked up by one of Paul's officers and took us to his headquarters in Pariack. During the supper, I realized that something was wrong, and I communicated this to Fr. William when we were going to sleep. He did not believe me, arguing that if an attack were imminent, Commander Paul would have told us. I told him that we were civilians and that it was not appropriate to inform us of military matters. There was a lot of movements of the artilleries and vehicles including the one tank that I had previous seen with Kerubino in Marial Baai before he rejoined the movement he spearheaded. Fr. William said let's say our bed time prayers and God will take care of the rest. I agree and we said our prayers.

The following morning, Commander Paul informed us about the imminent attack by militias. He gave us bicycles to escape with because all the vehicles he had would be used to fight the militia forces and protect the civilians of Warawar. Fr. William told me to go and get my sister because he was expecting a flight the following day. World Vision's plane was on its way to pick up staff, so I told Fr. William to take this plane to Nairobi, where he lived. Fr. William refused, saying, "You brought your sister because we want her to go for treatment. And I cannot abandon her, because once I am gone the diocese, will not send a plane here — especially with the current situation."

Though I was grateful for his bravery and concern for my sister, I did not want him to die because of us. He told me to take the bicycle and go to Madhol, and return to Malual Kon the following morning. I left and went to Madhol, but it was not long after my arrival that people started running and saying that Arab militias were approaching on horseback to attack the citizens.

I put my sister on the bicycle and placed my own feet on the pedals. My sister fell off the bicycle twice, but I kept putting her back on and peddling. The fear on people's faces was so great that my sister insisted I leave her and run. She argued that she was sick and it would be better if she alone died instead of both of us dying. She expected that the latter situation would end our family because our mother and other sister would die of heart attacks. I refused to leave her and kept pedaling while she sat at the back. She was crying, begging me to leave her and run. I ran out of patience and yelled at her to shut up!

I do not believe there is anybody in this world with a sound mind that would abandon their own sister and run. I said, "If it was our fate to die together on this day, and then let it be." When she could not keep quiet, I did not answer her back. We managed to reach a place in the forest deemed safe by the people there in the area of Madhol. About an hour later, we learned that SPLM/A forces had repelled the attackers and that the militias never made it into the city. We went back to Madhol and spent the night there. I prayed to the spirit of our father, who always listens to me in times of need. Jesus and his Father have billions of people to listen to and help, but our father looks over us and immediately answers our prayers.

The following morning, I put my sister on the bicycle and went to Malual Kon, where I met the plane that came to pick up Fr. William. We then went to Marial Lou where Fr. William left and instructed us to see Fr. Matthew, an older Italian priest who offered us a room in the church compound upon his return.

At Marial Lou, suffering greeted us at the airstrip, and the reality of famine sank in deeply. As soon as we arrived in Marial Lou, starvation was everywhere. People were dying daily by the dozens. There was neither local nor foreign media present to report on the tragedy. I realized the ugliness of war. Signs of brutality, callousness, and cruelty greeted me wherever I went.

The Catholic Church was the only relief distributor in the area, which had planes coming with food every Monday and Wednesday. In addition to being a teacher in Marial Lou, I was also a relief distributor. I took this as an opportunity to serve my people. At the end of August, 1998, Fr. Mathias, an Italian Roman Catholic parish priest in Marial Lou, wrote a note asking me to give one of the commanders in the area eight sacks of sorghum. I refused, saying I would give him six sacks on Monday and two on the following Wednesday. There was no way I would give one person that many sacks of sorghum while more than twenty children and women were starving to death on that day.

When the commander learned what I did, he was furious and wanted to kill me. This captain, a commander, accused me of being a "nygat" because I was from the area of Kerubino. I thought that being an SPLM/A captain was not a license to receive better services, but I was dead wrong. When I refused to favor this captain over the rest of the walking skeletons, the captain and his allies wanted to kill me. I was left with few options. The priest recommended that my sister and I flee to Kakuma, the refugee camp in Kenya.

The commander ordered his bodyguards to kill me whenever they could do so without the knowledge of the public. Even though Kerubino was jailed without trial for a very long time, the fact that he was forced to join the Khartoum government made him an enemy to the very movement he started. I didn't want the same thing to happen to me.

There was a division in the camp between the captain who wanted to kill me and the people who defended me; the people were mostly from the captain's home area. Some of his soldiers rejected the order and split the camp. When the priest learned about this, he wanted to stop all relief distributions, and it took me a full day to persuade him to change his mind. He then privately arranged for my sister and I to go to Kenya, without even alerting me, for fear that the commander would find out and kill me before my sister and I could leave the area.

However, before this could happen, a soldier came one night and knocked on our door, saying I must come out or he would shoot me and my sister. I told him I was going to come out and talk to him. Instead, I opened the door half way but I did not come out, and so he entered instead. I threw him down and kept him with all my strength. I then took control of his gun. Luckily, he was drunk, so it did not take long. I sent my sister to call for help since it was still at night, and since the parish compound was nearby, my sister alerted a group of seminarians. These seminarians came to assist us and some of them wanted to harm the soldier but I refused. I had to get full information regarding why he wanted to kill me. The seminarians agreed with me and we all became interrogators. The soldier confessed that the captain sent him because he, the captain, wanted me dead.

I began weighing my options: shoot him in self-defense, or risk letting him kill us if he got his gun back. Killing him would also help the captain kill me. When I had enough young men from the church compound at my side, I gave him his gun back with assurances that he was not going to use it against me. After getting full information from him, I told the seminarians to let him go.

The attacker became apologetic when, instead of shooting him, I gave back his gun and told him to go. Few days later, the attacker came to my house with his three friends. I offered them tea and some soups that my sister had made for me before they arrived. His friends asked me what happened the night Majok came to attacked me. I told them I did not know Majok's name until then but I explained to them exactly what happened. One of his friends asked why let him go instead of shooting since he came to kill me. I replied that God saved me and there was no reason for me to kill him. I am called Abuna for a reason. Abuna is an Arabic word for pastor or priest. I had my education in seminary with intention to become a priest, all what I learned from seminary is Jesus: did not only teach his disciples to forgive but lived through his life. I took that opportunity to preach to them what I believe.

Majok, the man who attacked me, as I learned his name, could not believe it, and became my friend who informed me what the captain was up to. His information saved my life. A week before my sister and I left for Kenya, Majok reported that captain had paid two soldiers to kill me. I called two friends of mine to be witnesses to what he said and I warned him of the consequences if he were lying to me. I said, I would report the very captain. My intention was to find out exactly if he was telling a lie to get some food items in return. He sworn saying, "This is not lie" and he knew about the consequences of his action telling the plan. I brought and introduced him to the parish priest, who was at first very upset with him. But, as time went on, the priest appreciated the vital information this young soldier was providing regarding the moves of the captain against the church personnel in Marial Lou.

It became apparently clear that the captain mobilized some soldiers against me. He wanted to make sure I do leave Marial Lou. In addition to the information, Majok was providing, priest asked one of the parishioners he trusted to do his own independent research and the parishioner report was not different from what Majok had reported many times earlier. The priest secretly planned our trip to Kenya. My sister and I only came to know about our trip to Kenya two hours before the plane arrival. The priest did not want the captain to know for fear he will speed up his plan to kill me.

Hundreds of people died in Marial Lou, punctuating the brutality of the civil war, famine and inaction of those who could have averted these tragedies. The famine in Bahr el Ghazal region was caused by the government of Sudan, which blocked any United Nations logistics teams from entering the South. In my presence, hundreds of people, especially children, women, and the elderly, starved to death between the first week of June and the second week of September, 1998. This tragedy will always live with me.

Most of the bodies were not properly buried. Police officers called people to collect and bury the dead. These people were in no better shape than the bodies they were ordered to lay down to rest. The difference was that these people were breathing and the others were not. Sometimes the bodies were eaten by hyenas. Dinka tradition would have the dead buried in the household amongst their deceased ancestors. There are no graveyards in villages. Even Dinka in big cities take their departed loved ones to the village of their birth for a proper burial.

During those terrible days, I was in Marial Lou, where ten to fifteen people died every day. The officers ordered able-bodied men to dig graves about a quarter meter deep. The worst thing was not only the starvation of hundreds, if not thousands, but the fact that no national or international media was around to report it. The deaths were not reported on inside or outside of Sudan.

To make things worse, a lot of individuals in the very movement that set out to make life better for our people ended up caring only for themselves, their relatives, and their friends. This tragedy was incomprehensible to me, and I again questioned the altruism of humanity. Amidst all this, the revolutionary army commanders in the area did nothing to help their own people. I came to conclusion that some members of the SPLM/A neither they misunderstood the objectives of the moment or they were not better than the government they were fighting against. This became clear when I taught in the only elementary school run by Catholic diocese of Rumbek among malnourished people.

In addition to being an elementary school teacher, I was also working as Catholic Church Relief Personnel at Marial Lou Parish, from June 6 to September 12, 1998. I remember that time very well. The planes brought relief supplies every Monday and Wednesday. One Monday, the relief plane brought only cooking oil and the priest did not want us to give it out because to him, there was nothing could be done with oil. However, I insisted arguing that women would cook tree leaves with the oil. The priest reluctantly gave in, so I asked people to line up as usual and distributed the oil.

Unfortunately, my persuasion of the priest turned tragic. One of the children found the oil in a cup and drank it. When some teachers and I went to the school later, we found a dead child with oil coming out of every hole on his body: the nose, mouth, ears, and even his private parts. The boy had nothing in his stomach when he drank the oil so he died from this oil. This has lived with me ever since, and will continue to live with me. The priest and others in the parish talked to me many times, trying to convince me that it was not my fault. It is true that my intention was good, but I sometimes feel responsible for his death even though there was possibility he would had starved to death away.

The government of Sudan neither provided food, nor did it allow international agencies to assist the South Sudanese people. The boy's death and the deaths of thousands of South Sudanese were the direct result of Khartoum's efforts. The government blocked aid to Bahr el Ghazal because it was home to many Dinka, the chief SPLM/A sympathizers. The United Nations was banned from delivering food to Bahr el Ghazal, which was also a punishment to Kerubino and his forces for returning to the revolution that Kerubino had originally spearheaded.

In addition to teaching in Marial Lou, I worked as a relief supplies distributor and as a health-care worker for *Medicines Sans Frontiers* (Doctors Without Borders). I was even giving injections to babies as young as one week old! When I refused at first because I was scared and untrained, one of the doctors told me that I was a university student and most of his health care workers had only completed grades three or six. I had no choice but to work there and continue to vaccinate sick babies and administer drugs as directed by the nurse.

There is one big difference between the death of the boy from Marial Lou and the death of Alan, the three-year-old

Syrian who drowned and washed up on the shores of Europe. When Syrians flooded European countries, it became an international embarrassment. When Alan, his five-year-old sibling, Ghalib, his mother, and eight others drowned, their deaths went viral and big things happened for Syrian refugees. Canadian Prime Minister Justin Trudeau campaigned on the promise to bring 25, 000 Syrian refugees to Canada before the end of 2015, and won.

No media covered the death of that poor boy in South Sudan. He never received any cultural or dignified burial. I will never forget the preventable death of that boy as well as all those who died in Marial Lou under my watch. I shamefully admit that I did not know the boy's name. The boy's parents had starved to death two days earlier. At that time in Marial Lou, the deceased were not mourned, because everyone knew it was simply a matter of time before his or her loved ones died.

Children dying from preventable diseases are unfortunate and represent immoral neglect by those who could prevent these horrible situations. The death of this boy and many others made me question Carl Sandburg's wisdom that says, "A baby is God's opinion that the world should go on." If children were really God's opinion that the world should exist, then God must have a proper explanation for why children starve to death.

Due to that experience, I had questions but no answers. My questions include, "Why did God create and send these innocent souls to suffer in this world? Why did God allow children to starve to death, really?" These questions defeat my faith. Neither my African traditional religion nor my Catholicism could adequately provide an answer to these questions. At my crossroads of faith, no theological explanation can sufficiently explain to me why these tragic phenomena happen. However, I escape to Christian faith that says, one cannot understand God's plans. Even though I do not understand why these things happen, I seek refuge in God's mercy and compassion.

When the war in Wau interrupted my post-secondary education, my hope of completing university abruptly ended. Despite all the effort I had put into my education, I had no papers to prove my merit. On September 12th, 1998, my sister and I left for Kenya, where both of us became refugees.

Chapter 7

Life in a Refugee Camp

Out of human tragedies they come from
all corners of the world with a single goal
of seeking refuge, a safe space where they
can lick their wounds.[9]

A refugee lives between some undesired past and an
unknown future. I was in a refugee camp and had little
hope. Refugees worldwide are deprived of their country
of origin and often from their human rights. As a refugee
between 1998 and 2000, I lived between a past that I did
not want to remember and a desired unknown future. I
did not want to recall times when death was close by and
when children were dying of starvation. I wanted a future
of opportunities where I would be in charge of my destiny.

In any refugee camp, refugees live in the past or in the
future. They detest their refugee status. Refugees are in
a constant search of where to belong. I was no different.
Spending a year and three months in a refugee camp taught
me a valuable lesson. In a refugee camp, one's knowledge
does not matter.

---

[9] Maey Jo Leddy, working with refugees in Toronto, Canada.

The Kakuma Refugee Camp settlement in northwest Kenya was established in 1992 and was home to about 96, 000 refugees, according to a headcount I conducted in 2000. Kakuma provided shelter, food, water, and health services to refugees from Sudan, Somalia, Ethiopia, Burundi, Rwanda, the Democratic Republic of Congo, Eritrea, and Uganda. Refugees felt like prisoners, because we were not allowed to go to other towns in Kenya without a permit from the UN mission at the camp.

In the Kakuma refugee camp, I had no country to call home. This is because I was not a citizen of any country. I was born and raised in the Sudan, but at that time, I was not a Sudanese citizen. Neither was I a Kenyan citizen, although I lived in Kenya. Since I was stateless, I had no rights or privileges. I was a person without citizenship. A citizen, according to Peggy McIntosh, "possesses duties, rights, responsibilities, and privileges in a given political entity that demands loyalty from that individual while providing protection in return."[10] I had none of those benefits.

I did not have rights, privileges, duties, responsibilities or obligations and indeed had no clear protection when I was a refugee. No government could protect us other than the United Nations with its limited powers. The UN High Commissioner for Refugees (UNHCR) ran the camp with the help of the International Organization for Migration (IOM), the World Food Program (WFP), the Lutheran World Federation (LWF), the International

---

[10] Noddings, Nel. *Educating Citizens for Global Awareness*, 2005, p. 22

Rescue Committee (IRC), Jesuit Refugee Services (JRS), the National Council of Churches of Kenya (NCCK), Windle Trust Kenya (WTK), and Don Bosco of Kenya.

The housing was inadequate and the food was unacceptable; yet, the refugees shared the little we had with newcomers to the camp. On September 12th, 1998, when my sister and I arrived in the evening, at about 5:00 p.m., we did not know anyone in the camp nor was there a motel in the camp. The people we asked directed us to where people from my home area lived. One of the surprising things about the camp was that it was divided into groups. The camp was not only divided on tribal lines, but according to the village people initially came from. We were taken to the home of our distant uncle, Atem Majok Atem.

In this house, Isaac Bith Madut Kunyjok and his family welcomed us. Although I had never met any of these family members, our introduction to the people of the house assured us of our safety. Despite the warm welcome and hospitality extended to us, Kakuma's hostile environment and many difficulties became a daily struggle for us. I thought my sister and I would stay there for a couple of months. We never thought we would be there for more than a year. However, my stay there gave me a glimpse into what refugees go through. Despite difficulties in the camp, everyone in the camp hoped that he or she would go to a better place, someday. The hope was that life would be better. Refugees hope that they will be resettled by United Nations to developed nations.

On September 14, 1998, two days after my arrival in

the Kakuma Refugee Camp, I went back to Loki to get my documents. They were taken by prominent South Sudan politician from Twic, Bona Malwal Madut. This was my first encounter with Kenyan police at outpost. When the mini we were on arrived, one of the police officers said, "All Dinka must get out of the mini bus." I did not get down with others. I kept on reading a newspaper I had. As one of these officers came to see if there was any Sudanese left, he saw me and said pointing at me, "Get down." I replied, "I am a Sudanese." "That is what I meant," the police officer answered. I corrected him that Dinka is just one of the tribes in the Sudan. I wanted to show the police that not all Sudanese are Dinka. Dinka is only one of the tribes in the Sudan, like Kenya has Turkana and many other tribes. I wanted to prove to that officer that he was wrong to call all Sudanese Dinka. This to me was a sign of ignorance. I had to come down finally after lengthy argument which upset some Sudanese because they were used to it and to them I was wasting their time.

The police officer asked for my immigration document which I produced. He told me he wanted me to support my document. I asked "What do you mean by supporting my documents? He said, "Friend, where are you coming from? "I am from Sudan", I responded, he became agitated pulled me aside and said something in Kiswahili which I did not understand. I insisted that I was legally residing in Kenya. He asserted, "You fool, why you don't understand." One of the passengers asked me in Dinka to pay something to the police. These police officers will not let us go, so please give them anything. When I became adamant about it, this man gave some me to the police and the police sworn at me in Kiswahili. One of the officers told the driver of the mini bus to go. I went to Loki and came back to Kakuma after two days.

I stayed in Kakuma Refugee Camp from 1998—2000. Life in the camp was very hard, with hopelessness visible in the eyes of countless men, women, and children. Everyone was just a refugee. In the camp, your prior knowledge is nothing and does not count at all. I wanted to do something for myself as well as for the refugees especially the women that had nothing to do in the camp.

I asked around about who run the camp. I was told it was United Nations High Commissions for Refugees. So, one month after my arrival in Kakuma Refugee Camp, I got involved in a new program run by the LWF, which was charged with education and initiating a women's literacy program, and I became one of its two first teachers. In less than a month, the program registered more than three hundred women who were happy to learn. I always believed that women's empowerment is the way forward and that it will help solve many problems that exist in the camp.

One of my motivations to educate women is that empowering them will later provide our country with needed peace and stability. I was able to tell my story and demonstrated that age is not a hindrance to education. I told these women who were attending the evening class that when I began my education, I only wanted to learn how to read and write my name. I encouraged them that if they wanted they would be able to learn how to read and write.

The fact that I started my elementary school at an older age made me a strong believer that age should not prevent anyone from acquiring a formal education. After two months of teaching women, young and old, I was offered a teaching position by the LWF under the UNHCR at Napata Secondary School. As a high school teacher, I could connect with many students. Most students were my age or older.

Most of my students later resettled in the United States of America. They were part of the Lost Boys and Lost Girls of Sudan, beginning in 2000. These boys and girls became appointed ambassadors to the USA. I call them appointed ambassadors because no government appointed them to represent the oppressed people of Southern Sudan, but their stories aroused the interests of the American people to support the movement and the people of Southern Sudan to achieve their hard-fought independence.

As refugees, we had unsubstantiated hope to keep us going on when things were not good in the camp. Sometimes unsubstantiated hope can be a source of strength in desperate situations. I clearly remember a soldier from Dar Fur, whose one limb was amputated, named Mohammed Hassan Ali, who always entertained us in Kakuma. Ali used to say that the American people are all moving to another planet that they discovered. According to him, going to America meant going to heaven, because there would be no work to do. In America, as he comforted desperate refugees, everything was already prepared.

Those chosen to go to America, he told us, were lucky because they would only enjoy what Americans had left behind. Although most refugees knew that was not the case, it fed people with hope that things would change for the better. The truth that was buried and never talked about was the America that we called "heaven on earth" was built by African slaves. Though times have changed, these boys and girls still had no choice but to go to the land of the American dream.

According to Ali, refugees would inherit everything in America. Every time Ali spoke, everyone would listen attentively to him. He usually began by saying, "Listen up, we refugees will inherit all that Americans labored for, including vehicles, houses and everything." Wallai Allahizim added, "I dreamt about this last night, and believe me, it is true."

When Ali spoke, people who were suffering from malnutrition and lack of a country to identify with started to believe him, especially when America began taking Lost Boys and Girls. In its infancy, we heard, American capitalism needed black labour, but now the Americans were evacuating and leaving everything behind for another planet.

All refugees hang on to hope, but hope only works when there are people ready to help support that hope with tangible things. Things like having access to education or employment opportunities. Ali's story was that Americans were offering their country and all their belongings to the refugees to inherit. I do not remember how Ali came up with this theory, but it seemed to sink well with refugees who would believe anything to alleviate their sufferings in the camp.

Ali's story resonated with refugees, because as a refugee, you lose your previous identity and find yourself looking forward to a new one. People need a secure country in which to recreate their own identity and shape the future of the country. In South Sudan, this would mean creating a life that is free from preventable suffering. This reminds me of the story in the book called *Animal Farm*. In this book, there is someone called Moses who always talked about the sugar cane in the sky. In Animals' Farm, Moses story kept the rest of the animals working hard with hope that one day they will arrive at the place of sugar. Ali's story kept people going in difficult times, even though they knew it was not true.

In a refugee camp, there is no immediate government except for the United Nations. The UN is now comprised of 193 countries, but a small few decide what will be done. These few sit on the powerful UN Security Council and enjoy veto power. The UN is a community where some the United States, China, France, Russia, and Great Britain are more equal than others. Only these five countries can veto anything that threatens their interests. We South Sudanese in camp at the time blamed Russia, France, and China for blocking many attempts to sanction Sudan for its actions.

Even in a refugee camp, the strength of unity of refugees becomes a force that the UNHCR has to reckon with. My thoughts go back to the refugee camp in general, and to the teachers' strike that we had in Kakuma in particular. When the kindergarten, primary, and secondary school teachers began to strike, I found myself in the lead: I was leading the strike.

There were thousands of South Sudanese and people from six other countries in the camp. Although the majority had been there since 1992, they still could not access the resettlement services. I am grateful that I was resettled in Canada, but there were people in much greater need than me, yet they were not chosen. Whenever refugees are blessed enough to get another chance, they start from zero.

Life in a refugee camp can be compared to the journey of the biblical Israelites in the wilderness. When the Israelites spent forty years in the wilderness, they believed that God was their only protector. For us refugees, the UNHCR was our protector, despite all its imperfections. The UNHCR depends on the generosity of the developed nations to effectively carry out its duties and deliver services to the refugees.

As it remains for millions of refugees worldwide, hope was my strength in Kakuma Refugee Camp. My hope was borne out when I came to Canada, which has been a golden opportunity for me. I believe that Canada offers similar opportunities to all new immigrants despite the challenges they encounter. Though we are all born with our own unique abilities, we still need the support and opportunities provided by a country like Canada to pursue and realize our dreams in supportive environment.

While in the refugee camp, I knew that my chances of

achieving my dreams were very slim. In the camp, my former education and experiences did not matter much. After all, I was just a refugee. I hung on to hope. The problem is, I had something else to blame: refugee life for not providing opportunities for life. Now that I am in Canada and no longer have the immediate stresses of living in a refugee camp, any of my failures will be my own fault. Sometimes this worries me. Sometimes, it is hard to make good choices. Choice between assisting my extended relatives back or work to provide better future for my children.

When the civil war disrupted my education, there were few opportunities, and my hope for acquiring a university degree was getting dimmer day by day. I realized that I needed to complete my education by any means necessary, but being a refugee was a great disadvantage. My applications were accepted at Day Star University and Catholic University but I had no money for tuition. To solve this problem, I applied to World University Service of Canada for a scholarship.

When I received the news that I was accepted to the University of Regina in the province of Saskatchewan, Canada, I was very glad. Not only could I complete my unfinished post-secondary education, but I would also get a second chance at life, thanks to Canada and the WUSC. Yet, even though I was running away from Sudan, I could not ignore my strong desire to return one day after I had completed my education.

During my interview with a Canadian immigration lawyer at the Canadian embassy in Nairobi, in 2000, I asked if I could ever return to Sudan. The interviewer said yes, "You would whenever you want." He asked me if I had another question but I did not. To my relief and delight, he gave me his hand and congratulated me. I would be going to Canada.

CHAPTER 8

HOME AND AWAY: NEITHER HERE NOR THERE

> You are now entitled to all the rights
> and privileges of Canadian Citizenship
> and are subject to all the obligations and
> responsibilities of your citizenship.[11]

Immigrants from war-torn countries grapple with the issues of dual citizenship. Canada offers numerous opportunities that enable me to nourish my dreams. Within a short time after my arrival, I was able to pay off the loan I took out to buy my airplane ticket. I also had to choose between pursuing education and making money to support family members, relatives, and friends back home and in refugee camps. I chose the former, a decision that might have disappointed some relatives and friends, especially those who were in a dire situation and wanted financial support. I disappointed them by choosing education over making money. In addition to the dissatisfaction of relatives and friends, I have some reconciling to do: I have not only to reconcile my Atemyath faith with Christianity, but also to

---

[11] Judy Sgro, Minister of Citizenship and Immigration of Canada on the day I became Canadian citizen, 2004.

find harmony between Canadian values and Dinka values (such as the importance of polygamy and ghost marriages). Some these problems are faced by almost all new immigrants from developing nations, including those who do not leave due to a war. However, the challenges that new immigrants face in Canada are outweighed by the opportunities and security we get.

Even those who choose to support the family members back home also face disappointments from those they assist. The people still in South Sudan and refugee camps want their relatives who have resettled in the west to further their education.

When I was in Kakuma refugee camp in Kenya, many refugees considered Canada a promised land. To them, my arrival was like reaching the Promised Land. The question is "Who promised the land? In the Bible, God promised the Israelites land; in my case, it was hope that once I reach Canada, I will maximize every opportunity I get. Physically, I was in Canada, but mentally, my mind was still in Sudan thinking about what had happened and unable to know what was happening.

After two long years in the refugee camp without a country to call home, I now have both Canada and the Republic of South Sudan to call homes. The hopelessness I experienced in the refugee camp was now gone, but I came to Canada without any relatives, friends, or anyone from my home area. I felt lonely sometimes. In addition to homesickness, I had other worries. For example, in South Sudan, we live a communal life. Many South Sudanese who now live in the West are expected to help everyone back home. No one can blame these people, who have suffered from war and insecurity for many years, for their dependency. The majority depend on remittances sent from the family members and relatives in the diaspora.

Since I chose to further my education and turn my dreams into reality, I had and still have an unjustifiable fear. Secretly, I continue to fear that I cannot successfully integrate into Canadian society, even after becoming a Canadian citizen. I am afraid that new challenges I face in Canada may become obstacles to achieving my dreams. I am also afraid I will be seen as a foreigner in South Sudan, having become a Canadian citizen. Like many new immigrants, I struggle with the fear that I may not be able to meet the expectations of relatives and friends in refugee camps and back home in South Sudan. As I settled on campus of University of Regina, I could not leave behind my experiences.

One frigid winter day, in January, 2001, I sat by the window in my small, well-furnished room in the College West residence. I began to deeply think about what I and other Sudanese children went through. Among the questions that lingered in my mind that day was why the UN and the international community stood aloof and failed to save the South Sudanese children who were barbarically killed and enslaved.

Then, I remembered what my icon Cardinal Gabriel Zubeir Wako told me when I decided to go to Bahr El Ghazal University. He said to focus on my education instead of helping my relatives. His argument was, if I am educated, I will be able to help myself and then other people.

As a new immigrant to Canada, I began to worry about failing to achieve the hopes and dreams I had in the camp. I became worried about not meeting the expectations that family and friends had placed on me to support them. These expectations were common to most, if not all, new immigrants. It is an unavoidable dilemma that once you are resettled in the Western world, you are expected to solve many problems facing your people back home and in refugee camps. Again, given the experiences in Sudan and refugee camp, I cannot blame these people.

I had the strong inclination to go back to my country as soon as I finished my education. As time went on, I had to accept the reality that Canada is my home too. Adrienne Clarkson assures people like me when she writes, "You might feel that you have roots somewhere else, but in reality, you are right here with us." [12] Canada and South Sudan are both my homes. Minister of Immigration and Citizenship, Judy Sgro, echoed this on the day of my citizenship ceremony. On the next page is the document I received upon becoming a Canadian citizen.

One time I was teaching in a young offenders' prison, and I began to talk about my life. I told the students that I did not attend school before I was fifteen or sixteen years old, and yet, I have obtained two bachelor degrees. The

---

[12] Clarkson, Adrienne. Belonging The Paradox of Citizenship 2014, p. 6

message was that we should not let our scars determine our future. One of the young offenders then said to me, "Uncle Martino, you were not told at the age of two that you were good for nothing and beaten constantly at that age?" Students called me uncle not out of respect but because I joke with them. With that question, I was dumbfounded and began to realize that my life experience may not be the worst story after all. Aware of this, I said to myself there are people out here who have worse experiences than those in the so called third world countries, underdeveloped nations or developing ones — and that everyone's personal circumstances are different.

The youth's statement reminded me of Nelson Mandela's declaration in *Long Walk to Freedom*: "A nation should not be judged by how it treats its highest citizens, but its lowest ones." In the same book, Mandela says, "In South Africa, to be poor and black was normal; to be poor and white was a tragedy." My work in the Ministry of Justice of Corrections, Government of Saskatchewan, has left me with many unanswered questions. One question is whether to be poor and Aboriginal in Canada is normal, and to be poor and white is tragic. The answer to this question is for Canadians to consider.

When I acquired Canadian citizenship, I became more optimistic about realizing my dreams in achieving post-secondary education without any interruption. The truth is, I am torn apart by two nationalities and two different values. I sometimes find myself becoming an unofficial ambassador for both countries.

Even when I am entitled to all the rights and privileges of Canadian citizenship, I sometimes feel at home and away. I am home because I enjoy all the rights and privileges that my newly-acquired Canadian citizenship offers me; yet I miss my culture and the country that shaped my way of thinking. But even though I have roots somewhere else, I call Canada home. My Canadian citizenship brings me some sort of security and the promise of a better life. When in South Sudan, I become an unofficial and self-appointed ambassador for Canada. I defend Canadian values and culture.

I acquired all rights, responsibilities, obligations, and duties like all Canadians. In Canada, I defend the values and cultures of the Dinka in particular and South Sudanese culture in general. As a Christian, I defend and promote Christian values when in South Sudan. The only thing I never try to promote is my Dinka religion. This is because the Dinka do not have one deity but multiple divinities. Each clan has its own deity, and Dinka never attempt to convert others to their clan's deity. Only through marriage will that clan bring in new members.

When I became a Canadian citizen, I had to pledge allegiance to the Queen of England, a nation that left power entirely in the hands of Arabs in the North on Sudan independence, January 1st, 1956. As a Canadian citizen, I am ceremonially under the British monarchy, since the Queen is represented by Governor General. What a world we live in! My dual citizenship offers me the rights as well as the duties and obligations that come with citizenship under each country. As this book goes to print, Canada celebrates 150 years as a nation. The Republic of the South Sudan did not celebrate her six years of independence due to insecurity in the country.

Canada is one of the wealthiest countries in the world. If one works hard, the chances are fair that one can live a decent life. Although it is not a perfect or wholly just society, Canada is rich, full of opportunities, embraces multiculturalism, and respects people's sexual orientation, political affiliation, and all sorts of freedoms. Canada celebrates all these things. In South Sudan, ethnic groups are used by political elites for their personal gains, and in turn the civil war and its consequences destroy the new country. Our leaders of South Sudan have so far poorly managed national resources, manifestation shared by most African leaders.

Even after my father's death, I had all that a child needed according to the standards of the village and the country. I had the spiritual and emotional resources needed to survive, develop, and thrive. Atemyath and Kuonyath interceded for us whenever we needed them. Nhialic Madhol (God) was the Supreme Divinity. I enjoyed my cultural rights and would have achieved my full potential as an equal member of my original society had it not been for war.

In addition to being a citizen of two countries, I was brought up in Dinka culture where there were many deities. Each clan has its own deity symbolized by an animal, snake, or tree. Besides, Dinka people believe in the spirits of their ancestors. Dinka people share the belief in one God (Allah) and they call their God *Nhialic Mathdol* or *Nhialic Aciek* depending on which Dinka section one is born into.

When in danger, I also call upon the spirit of my father, who I believe protects his children. In the Roman Catholic Church, people ask for intercessions of Mary, the mother of Jesus, and of saints. One of the reasons, Mary the mother of Jesus intercedes when asked is because she is believed to be closer to Jesus than any other human being, and so are the saints.

I use two different lenses for my moral compass depending where I am. When I am in South Sudan, I defend Canadian values. In Canada, I defend Dinka values. The most challenging thing is making extremists from both countries understand the viewpoint of the other. Being a Canadian makes me a citizen of North America, while being a South Sudanese makes me a citizen of Africa. Therefore, I call myself a citizen of two continents.

My journey from Atamyath to Christianity, from Dinka values to Canadian values, sometimes makes me feel torn apart. But at other times it makes me feel blessed. Due to all of these, I have called myself an unofficial and self-appointed ambassador who defends Dinka values as well as Canadian values, despite the contradictions.

This is the author sitting in his room at College
West, U of R, contemplating his experiences.

I pondered and wondered to what happened to people
like Ring Atem (known as Abukdickgin) and Camilo who
disappeared in Sudan without a trace and many people who
were even killed by the very movement they created.

In the Sudan, people suspected of supporting the
SPLM/A were mostly murdered in cold blood while in the
SPLM/A, the struggle for power among the leaders led to
many deaths of the moment leaders. As I looked back at
my life, I also look forward to what my future holds for
me in Canada, a land of opportunities. South Sudan is the
country whose experiences made me who I am today. My
new home, Canada, offers me hope, fear, and challenges.
In Canada, I am hopeful that I will be able to raise my

children in peaceful environment. I am able to explore and take advantage of every opportunity Canada avails for me and my family.

Abukdickgin was a tall and handsome Dinka man, who spoke passionately about the movement. Among his crimes, Ring sang the SPLM/A morale songs, celebrating the aims and objectives of the rebel army. Abukdickgin was a victim because of his belief in a New Sudan, in which everyone would be treated as equals.

Abukdickgin disappeared from Kosti in 1987. Abukdickgin disappeared because he openly supported the rebellion, but he did not take up arms. He was a SPLM/A sympathizer. When Abukdickgin disappeared, everyone who knew him well was bewildered. Abukdickgin's crime was his bravery to challenge the status quo. He argued that if northerners wanted Sudan to stay united, they had to change their behavior. He predicted this on July 9th, 2011, when Sudan officially split into two nations.

What made Abukdickgin's disappearance more disturbing for me was not only that he was an innocent person killed for no reason, but also that he was from my home area of Twic. Ring Abukdickgin was a very friendly man. He was one of the few people who believed that age should not impede education. When people discouraged me because of my age, Abukdickin repeatedly told me not to take those people seriously. He emphasized that if I was willing to go to school, I should follow my heart's desire. Abukdickgin encouraged me to pursue an education when others told me that going to school at that age was a waste of time.

Empathizing with the rebels meant disaster for any southern Sudanese in government-controlled areas. Abukdickgin was supporting the objectives of the rebellion with all his heart in the belief that a New Sudan, in which everyone is treated fairly and equally, is possible. He argued with Arabs in Kosti, telling them that the SPLM/A had a real cause. Abukdickgin's family is not sure where he is, but his absence of more than three decade suggests that he was murdered in cold blood by the Khartoum regime's security apparatus.

Abukdickgin had a very strong personality. He was very tall and elegant. Abukdickgin was a few inches shorter than the late Manut Madut Bol, who was 7 feet tall. Both Manut Bol and Abukdickgin are from Twic. I recall when he used to tune into SPLM/A radio. The radio was the only way to receive information about the war and tell of the movement's successes. The stories broadcasted by SPLM/A's radio were never told in the Sudanese media. The other media outlet Abukdickgin listened to was the BBC English services radio, focused on Africa program. These were crimes that led to his disappearance and eventually his death.

Abukdickgin's vanishing was painful to bear for his family relatives and friends. Those of us who were living in Kosti at the time were hit hard with this news. Those of us in Kosti knew one of those security agents who kidnapped him at night in his residence. The agent used to come to the restaurant of my uncle Atem Abdul Karim, but no one questioned him out of fear. If anyone had dared question him, that person could have disappeared too.

The government murdered its very own citizens who questioned their policies towards southern Sudan. There were many people who vanished without a trace because of their political views. This is one of the reasons I celebrate my new country, Canada, where every political affiliation and opinion is respected. Political freedom is guaranteed by the Constitution of Canada and in the Charter of Rights and Freedoms.

As I was deeply contemplating and envisioning Abukickgin, my thoughts turned to another prominent southern Sudanese general who served in the Sudan's government against SPLM/A until he was tortured and died in the ghost house in Khartoum. Southern intellectual Camilo was killed by the Khartoum government that he had previously supported. That government used Southerners as long as they supported Sudan's government against the South, but as soon as these South Sudanese raised issues pertaining to how civilians in South Sudan are targeted, they were killed by government security operatives.

I vividly remember when Camillo came to the seminary in Kober-Khartoum and addressed the seminarians. Like many seminarians at the time, I saw in him strength and bitterness against the war in the South. Although I did not like his support for the Khartoum government, I liked his bravery. In my culture, bravery is valued, respected, and admired. When he spoke, I strongly remembered the bitterness my father had felt against Southern Sudanese who surrendered to the government in Anynya 1. While listening to Camilo, I wondered: if my father were alive, would he have supported the SPLM/A, or opposed it? I will never know the answer to this question. After a while, I realized those thoughts were irrelevant. My focus turned to whether South Sudan would one day become an independent nation.

In 2010, I left Canada for southern Sudan for the third time since I came to Canada. I was lucky to witness what millions of those southern Sudanese did not. I was there when South Sudan received her independence. I believed those who sacrificed their lives in order to have an independent South Sudan were glad in the world of ancestors. South Sudanese people will always be grateful to those who died fighting for full independence.

I did not sleep on July 8th, 2011, the night before the celebration of the new Republic of South Sudan. I wished my father was alive to witness this independence, something he had devoted his life to, even to the point of damaging his relationship with his father. It was painful for me, that my father had not lived long enough to share this joy with me and millions of South Sudanese worldwide. To me, this celebration was bliss, a dream my father did not live to see come true. I thought my father would have regained trust in his fellow South Sudanese, who managed to achieve what he and his colleagues in the Anynya 1 did not.

The joy of independence, was short-lived due to the belief of some SPLM members in the leadership that SPLM Party was inseparable from Republic of South Sudan. This belief is so strong that even prevalent of nepotism, corruption and lack of services delivery could not let them examine their unjustifiable faith that SPLM Party was everlasting savior of South Sudan.

CHAPTER 9

SPLM's Entitlement Syndrome

"The SPLM is a bloody party that has massacred its own people , lost popularity, vision, direction, and as such will never reunite its members and the entire nation of South Sudan", Gathoth Gatkuoth Hothyang. Nicholas Coghlan: Collapse of a Country: A Diplomate's Memoire of South Sudan, 2017, p. 176.

Without doubt, Sudan People's Liberation Movement/ Army dominated Sudan and Southern Sudan politics since its inception in 1983. It was a force that fought against four different governments in the Sudan. The civil war that SPLM/A waged in the Sudan and other factors led to the collapse of Jaafar Neimeiry's government in April 1985. Abdul Rahman Suwar ad-Dahhb seized power and fought against SPLM for a year before Sadiq al-Mahdi took over through general elections in which, areas under control of SPLM/A did not participate. When government of Sadiq al-Mahdi was about to clinch peace agreement with SPLM/A, Omer Bashir took power in bloodless coup, promising Sudanese people that his government was going to defeat the SPLM/A once and for all. Sixteen years later, Bashir's government signed Comprehensive Peace Agreement known as CPA with SPLM/A in January, 2005 after his government realized that SPLM/A was undefeatable force. In this agreement; the SPLM was to govern Southern Sudan for six years before Self-Determination referendum scheduled for January 2011. The strength that SPLM/A had shown to various governments of the Sudan allowed Southern Sudanese to vote in a referendum for Self-Determination in January, 2011. That vote resulted in independence for South Sudan, July 9th, 2011.

All the above mentioned reasons have led some SPLM members to believe that the Republic of South Sudan belongs to the SPLM. However, those reasons cannot and will never justify entitlement syndrome of these individual SPLM members. Since SPLM took over the rule of Southern Sudan and then Republic of South Sudan, the SPLM failed to deliver basic services to Southern Sudan, 2005-2011. During this period, corruption, nepotism and tribalism engulfed Southern Sudan.

Regrettably, the widespread corruption, nepotism and tribal based support for SPLM leaders did not end with the independence of South Sudan. All these combined with the SPLM party internal power struggle culminated into South Sudan's senseless and unjustifiable civil war in 2013. The civil war has proven beyond reasonable doubt that this entitlement syndrome has caused South Sudanese and continues to cause them thousands of lives and should be stopped. All South Sudanese must be equal regardless whether one participated in war militarily or not. The concept that we have liberated South Sudan only through guns and therefore, we must lead has not worked well since 2005 till now. It did not work and shall never work. It has become like Political Islam in the Sudan. Lasting peace, stability and prosperity can only be achieved when all South Sudanese become equal stakeholders in the country.

Nonexistence of services delivery and corruption did not end with the independence of South Sudan, so President Salva Kiir Mayardit in 2012, wrote a letter to seventy-five (75) officials that served in his government at various capacities, asking them to return some of more than four billions US dollars, they had embezzled. Unfortunately, instead of fixing the country, power struggle among SPLM' leadership became a tragedy to the new country.

A few years after independence, crisis emerged because of power struggles among our leaders, tribal conflicts, and corruption quickly sent the new country into a state of anarchy. Some friends of South Sudanese began to wonder whether we were ready to be a country. For an example, Hilde F. Johnson asserts that South Sudan became an abyss-like "country without a state." [13] My father's heart would have been shattered again, had he lived to see our politicians bringing the country to its knees due to a lust for power and wealth. Like many South Sudanese, I use social media to voice my disappointments regarding the way the country is being run.

---

[13] Johnson, Hilde F. South Sudan The Untold Story from Independence to Civil War. 2017, p. 17

Given the attitudes of some SPLM politicians, one would argue that these politicians are suffering from entitlement syndrome. For reasons known to them, they believe that South Sudan belongs to them. For an example, when the SPLM leadership created and executed merciless and ruthless civil war in 2013 and again 2016, the broke away SPLM under former Vice President Dr. Riek Machar still name itself the SPlM/A in Opposition while the one loyal to President Kiir Mayardit rename itself SPLM in government.

Forces loyal to President Kiir targeted and killed innocent Nuer ethnic group suspecting of supporting Dr. Riek Machar. The killing of civilians of Nuer tribe was carried out in the first few days of the war in Juba December 2013. The SPLM/A in Opposition targeted and killed innocent Dinka population under areas controlled by the opposition forces. People were killed in health care facilities, churches and even in UN camps in the country. The killing of innocent civilians by the SPLA forces on both sides amounts to genocides. These created enmity between the Dinka and Nuer tribes.

The killing of innocent Dinka by individuals from Equatoria especially on the roads and killing of people of Equatoria by some individuals in forces loyal to President Salva Kiir Mayardit created another enmity between Dinka tribe and the Equatorian region. The atrocities committed by all these forces have torn the nation apart. Failed policies of the ruling party and South Sudanese blind tribal and regional support are to blame for the catastrophes South Sudan is undergoing.

The Sudan leadership that wanted to impose Political Islam and Arabism did not succeed. The belief that every Sudanese must embrace political Islam and Arab culture was one of the main factors for civil wars in the Sudan prior to the independence of the Sudan and after. South Sudan separated and the civil war continues in various parts of the Sudan.

The problem of South Sudan is neither Dinka, Nuer, Bari, nor any particular ethnic group, but the belief that South Sudan and SPLM are inseparable is the problem, which is what I call "Entitlement Syndrome". The SPLM has failed the new nation and it can regain trust from South Sudanese if lasting peace, stability, equality and prosperity to the country are achieved in short time possible. Otherwise, it is time other parties can take over leadership of the nation through free and fair general elections.

Out of frustrations, I wrote open letters to the leaders of both the government and the armed opposition. Following are some of the letters I have sent to these political leaders.

Open Letter to Salva Kiir Mayardit, President of the Republic of South Sudan

April 20, 2015

Your Excellency,

On March 24th, 2015, the Parliament of Juba extended your Presidency for three more years. Well, there is nothing a mere citizen South Sudanese like me can do, but keep on voicing concerns. In the next three years, people expect from you and your administration drastic changes in regards to things like reduction of corruption.

People want to exercise their right to freedom of speech but few individual members of security agents intimidate people. For an example, on February 18, 2015, I directly sent you my statement entitled "Why President Salva Kiir Mayardit Must Go", before I posted it on social media (Facebook). I am not surprised if you did not get it because who am I to directly send my nonsense to the president of Republic of South Sudan. Well, I am one of the millions of South Sudanese people who elected you to presidency of Republic of South Sudan and made you and your government legitimate. Does this mean anything to you?

In December 5, 2012, Chan Awuol was gunned down outside his house in Gudele Juba because he called on you to stop supporting rebel groups fighting Khartoum. His view resulted into the embarrassing meeting of 21st September 2012, when President Obama shut down a meeting with you unceremoniously because you questioned the accuracy of his information. Thank you for releasing Peter Mayen, the leader of People Liberal Party and I hope you extend this good gesture to Kunayin Wek Mangarthi. Mr Mangarthi disappeared on February 9, 2015 and he is suspected to be illegally held by your security agents. Yet, some of your advisors are threatening Mr. Mangarthi's family members not to talk about his disappearance publicly. How can sound minded people be quiet when their loved one is nowhere to be found? I wish this was a movie, but the truth is that the family members of Mangarthi are in agony over his disappearance.

I still vividly remember the first handshake we had in your house in 2000, when you looked into my eyes and said, "You are welcome young man". Common citizens of South Sudan believe that you are a kind leader. Please, let your security agents release Mangarthi and all those in jail illegally. Your first priority should be guarding the democratic freedoms and security of all South Sudanese citizens.

There are two types of prisons in South Sudan. First prison is made up of the buildings where those who voice their rightful concerns about how you run the country are tortured and kept. These places of torture do not and will not help you, but create more enemies for you and your administration. I am not saying break down the prison cells nor do I suggest that you let people go without accountability. Those prisons should be for those who loot the resources as well as those who commit crimes against the constitution and the laws of the country.

The second type of prison is the prison of the mind. There are those who know very well that your administration implicitly condones corruption, but calling you on might become obstacles to their chances to serve in your government currently or in the future. Some might count on the opportunities that if and when they get into your government, they will do the same. These people oppress their conscience and their voice of reason and I totally get it. People who do not like criticisms unfairly label others as lacking respect to your administration. These people fail to realize that you are a politician and a statesman.

The people of South Sudan expect more actions on rampant corruption than words. You have talked tough on corruption in the country, but your words have not yielded anything. South Sudanese people are tired of rampant corruption and will never tolerate three more years of the same. On 3 May 2012, you wrote and signed a letter to 75 people who had served in your government at various levels asking them to return some of the stolen or embezzled funds amounted to $ 4 Billion to a secret account that you created on the conditions that their names will never be revealed to the public. You said in that letter "We fought for freedom, justice and equality". Your letter continues, "Many of our friends died to achieve these objectives. Yet, once we got to power, we forgot what we fought for, and began to enrich ourselves at the expense of others". I urge you to live by these statements.

The people who destroy your image and reputation are

those who make you allergic to criticism. You have taken public life and therefore, you have responsibilities to provide services to the people, especially those that need them most. Do not let few bad apples in the respected institution of National Security ruin your image, SPLM's image as well as of the country.

You fought for the people of South Sudan and so did the parents of those orphans in every corner of South Sudan. Their parents died fighting for the country we now call Republic of South Sudan. Do not be deceived by those who glorify your contributions so that they continue looting national resources with impunity. Your contribution to the liberation struggle should not be a license for them to bankrupt national treasures. Millions of war orphans have no access to schools, health care services, and those with single parents cannot afford a meal a day.

You have bought into it that the people in diaspora are your enemies. This is unfortunate. I put it this way in my previous post, "the people who started fighting in Juba on December 15, 2013 were not from diaspora…"

Please, take the extension of your term as an opportunity for you and your administration to fight corruption in its entirety. It also should be a chance for you to renew hopes, aspirations and dreams that South Sudanese had on July 9th 2011.

An Open Letter to President Salva Kiir Mayardit and First Vice President Dr. Riek Machar Republic of South Sudan

January 13, 2016

Ccs:

H. E. James Wani Igga, Vice President, Republic of South Sudan

SPLA, Gen Paul Malong Awan, General Chief of Staff

Your Excellences,

Criticizing either President Kiir or Dr. Riek without support from either side leaves one vulnerable before their diehard supporters. However, I have freely, consciously, and with no regrets chosen this lonely and dangerous route. Since November 8th, 2014, when I began to oppose President Kiir on the issue of two separate tribal armies and my subsequent public criticisms on some policies of his government, I have been labeled a rebel.

Your Excellency, Salva Kiir Mayardit, President of the Republic of South Sudan, most South Sudanese, including people who oppose some of your policies, agree that you are a good person. It is right time to consider the children and widows of those who died shielding you and your government in the brutal and ruthless civil war of South Sudan, 2013-2015. You and Dr. Riek Machar are the only people who can prevent other massacres like the one that just ended. Your apology of 7th, January, 2016, is in place because you are the president of the country, but your call on your supporters to vote for you in 2018 is declaration of destructions of lives and country again.

No doubt you want to be remembered for the years you spent fighting for your people in both civil wars of 1955-1972 and 1983- 2005. You want to be remembered as the first President of Republic of South Sudan, the leader who navigated a thick and dangerous path during implementation of The Comprehensive Peace Agreement (CPA) to deliver a country to the people of South Sudan, which you did July 9th, 2011. The nation will always be grateful for your patient style of leadership, which was tested many times by the National Congress Party (NCP), especially during the invasions of Abeyi in 2008 and 2011.

One of the best gifts you can offer yourself, your country and your people is to assure them that you will NOT contest in 2018 Presidential Election. During this period of Transitional Government of National Unity, I humbly beseech you to focus on creating an atmosphere for forgiveness, healing, reconciliation, and unity of your people, all 64 tribes. Our country is economically and politically on life support, but you and Dr. Riek Machar have power to perform the miracle that could rescue the Republic of South Sudan and make it a united, strong, and vibrant country.

Leaders who choose to relinquish power when their terms end, or for the interests of their country are globally revered and respected. For example, Nelson Mandela is admired globally as world icon not only because he spent

27 years in hard labor but also he relinquished power after serving only one term in the office as president. Thabo Mbeki, former President of South Africa, helped SPLM and NCP during the implementation of the CPA, and now, Botswana's former president, Festus Mogae, is ruling our nation indirectly during IGDA Plus Comprehensive Peace Agreement (CPA), Jimmy Carter served one term as president of America and has since done more humanitarian work worldwide than most of American presidents. I am sure you will make the right decision not because someone of no importance like me said it, but in the interests of your people and country.

I hope the statement posted by Sudantribune.com about your intention to run in 2018 is not true. Please, think about all those people who offered their ultimate sacrifices in order to keep you in power in December 2013 for about 22 months.
Please, do not accept the advice of those who want to loot the nation through your presidency.

Your Excellency, First Vice President Dr. Riek Machar Teny, you want to be remembered as a person who, after completing a PhD, abandoned the luxuries that accompany such higher academic achievements and chose to fight for and help his people. You want to be remembered as the South Sudan Vice President who raised the nation's flag in New York at the United Nations in 2011.

You and President Kiir can save South Sudan, or destroy it again, if either of you choose to, but there is no doubt in my mind that you will declare that you are NOT running for the 2018 Presidential Elections in order to honor those who sacrificed their lives in order to make you the first vice president. In December 2013, you left Juba with no power but people (one may call them Nuer) sacrificed their lives and that is why you are more powerful than when you were vice president 2010-2013. This will be the best gift, not only to the widows and orphans of your supporters, but also to the entire South Sudan. Dr. Riek declaring that he will not run for presidency 2018! What a memorable legacy, Dr. Riek!

October 5th 2015, in your address to South Sudanese in Kansas City, USA, my presence was acknowledged as a South Sudanese political activist, thanks to whoever gave my name to the master of ceremony, but I consider myself as an ordinary concerned South Sudanese Citizen. On May 20, 2015 and November 22nd, 2015 I declined two proposed positions in your movement because my criticisms of President Kiir's administration did not mean automatic support for you, nor was it about getting a position. It was all about having a country to call home.

For the sake of all those who sacrificed their lives, for their loved ones left behind, as well as for those who would die if another civil war erupted because you want to be president of South Sudan, I am sure you will make right decision by not running for presidency in 2018 elections. It is the right time for both of you, yourself and President Kiir, to step aside in order to help your people forgive each other, and yourselves, to assist them in building an environment for peaceful co-existence in a prosperous, united Republic of South Sudan, in which South Sudanese trust one another.

Fellow South Sudanese, the only way to avert other massacres is through forgiveness and reconciliation. As we all know, the callous and merciless civil war of 2013- 2015 was mainly about the power struggle between President Kiir Mayardit and Dr. Riek Machar. One group wanted to keep President Salva Kiir in power at all costs, while another group wanted to bring Dr. Riek Machar to power by force, in the process innocent Dinka and Nuer people died in larger numbers than any tribe in the country. I implore all South Sudanese to stop using tribes or regions for personal interests. Let's embrace the notion of "South Sudanism" where we all feel equal regardless of the number of one's tribe.

The truth of the matter is that there are more Dinkas who have access to Dr. Riek Machar than majority of Nuers. There are many Nuer who have more access to President Kiir than majority of Dinka. So let be clear, last civil war was not between Dinka and Nuer people, but between President Kiir and Riek. Unfortunately, innocent Dinka and Nuer were murdered in cold blood.

Revenge and counter revenge, will destroy lives and the country, as we have already witnessed. Both our leaders will make the right decision to not run in 2018 elections. Please, let's put our efforts together and collectively support them to prepare the nation for free and fair general elections in 2018 without them contesting the presidency. In our different capacities, let's rally support from International Community to assist our leaders so that they are able to build strong institutions for real democracy.

President Salva Kiir Mayardit and first Vice president Dr. Riek Machar, I humbly remind both of you that neither of you will ever again unite our people as president after that atrocious civil war.

Thank you, President Salva Kiir Mayardit and First Vice-President Dr. Riek Machar Teny.

CHAPTER 10

AFRICA IS A CONTINENT, NOT A COUNTRY

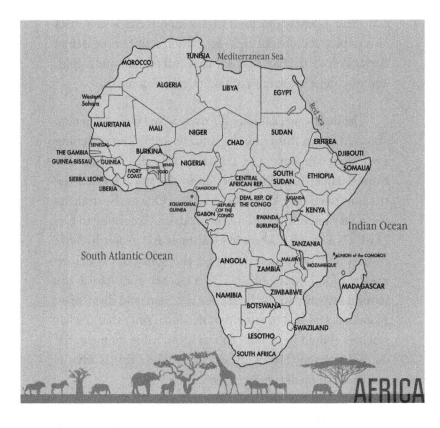

I include a map of Africa and a short note because of my teaching experience and interactions with Canadians. Some people refer to Africa as though it were a country. Africa is the second largest continent after Asia. Wars, poverty and bad leadership in Africa have influenced how Africa is viewed worldwide.

The legacy of colonialism and African leaders' mismanagement of resources have shattered the continent and overshadowed her beauty. Africa is full of rainforests, plains, mountains, jungles, and wildlife. The African continent is always in need of aid, and western countries always play the saviour role. Starvation and famine define Africa despite the fact that Africa is full of diamonds, gold, and oil. These are rarely seen on television screens.

The following examples illustrate why I included a note about Africa in this book. In January, 2015, I was teaching grade four students, and the story we were reading was from Ghana. As an introduction to the story, I asked the students what they knew about Africa. One of the students had a very interesting definition of Africa. According to her, "Africa is a country where wild animals and people live side by side. In Africa people do not get enough food to eat. They get their food from garbage." As a teacher from Africa, my natural response would have been defensive and dismissive. Nonetheless, I had to remain professional since that is what teachers should be. I took this as a teachable moment. Of course, I cannot blame my student because this is what is presented in media and western culture.

The student's perception is partially true, because many Africans do depend on foreign aid and donations. Africa is the continent with the worst poverty, so it would be unfair to totally dismiss what she claimed to know. However, her comment allowed me to tell the class about other things that Africa offers to the world. Although the lesson was not about Africa, I took that opportunity to teach my students that Africa is not all about starving children. I told my students that Africa is a continent of approximately 15 per cent of the earth's arable land. Tropical Africa alone has more than five hundred million hectares of land for agricultural development.

Another bold student provided an interesting answer to what Africa was. He said, "I know why you are here." Eager to know, I asked the student. "What?" "You are here because of Ebola. You guys eat monkeys and that is why you get Ebola." Again, my professionalism took charge and I began to tell the student that I came here before he was born. I explained to him and the whole class, that Africa is not a country, but a continent with fifty-four (54) countries.

When I asked my student where he learned that all Africans got Ebola from eating monkeys, he innocently stated his mother told him. This surprised me. A couple of weeks later, the mother of that child came to school for a three-way-conference. I never thought of telling the mother what her son told me, but I kept laughing for no apparent reason in the meeting. I would have explained to the mother that not all Africans eat monkeys, but this would have betrayed my student. Fearing what the mother would do her son soon once she returned home, I kept this information to myself. Incidents like these are the reasons I included a map of Africa, demonstrating the obvious, that Africa is a continent and not a country.

This is Atem's first book. After escaping the war-torn Southern Sudan to Northern Sudan, Atem attended evening schools, St. Augustine's minor seminary and St. Paul's national major seminary. He then, briefly studied at Bahr El Ghazal University, Wau Southern Sudan.

In 1998, Atem became a refugee in Kenya. In 2001, he received a scholarship to University of Regina through

World University Services of Canada. Atem holds a Bachelor of Arts in Philosophy and Religious Studies and a Bachelor's degree in Education with concentration on Social Studies, both from University of Regina. He currently teaches in the Regina Public School system. Since 2011, Atem has been working in Ministry of Justice, Corrections and Policing, Government of Saskatchewan.

Atem's volunteer work includes Secretary for Campion College Students' Association University of Regina, and Representative for International Students on President's Advisory Committee on Prevention of Harassment and Discrimination, University of Regina. He is currently the President of South Sudanese Association in Regina Inc., Saskatchewan-Canada.

Printed in the United States
By Bookmasters